Writing Well

Write,
Revise,
Succeed!

Libby Wilson

GED Teacher
Greater Erie Community Action Committee
Stairways Behavioral Health, Inc.

GED Trainer
Pennsylvania Bureau of Adult Basic and Literacy Education

New Readers Press

Dedicated to all adult education students, with hope that this book will encourage them to persevere in their educations. Never, ever give up!

Writing Well
Write, Revise, Succeed!

Libby Wilson
GED Teacher
Greater Erie Community Action Committee
Stairways Behavioral Health, Inc.

GED Trainer
Pennsylvania Bureau of Adult Basic and Literacy Education

ISBN 978-1-56420-557-5

New Readers Press
Division of ProLiteracy Worldwide
1320 Jamesville Avenue, Syracuse, New York 13210
www.newreaderspress.com

Printed in the United States of America
9 8 7 6 5 4 3 2

All proceeds from the sale of New Readers Press materials support literacy programs in the United States and worldwide.

Acquisitions Editor: Beth Oddy
Design and Production Manager: Andrea Woodbury
Illustrations: Linda Tiff, James Wallace, Carolyn Boehmer
Production Specialist: Jeffrey R. Smith
Cover Design: Kimbrly Koennecke

Contents

About This Book

What Is Writing?

How would you define writing? Is it spelling words correctly? Using correct grammar? Adding commas? Writing five paragraphs, including an introduction and a conclusion? Writing may include these, but it is much more. Writing is expressing your thoughts on paper so that someone else can understand them. The first goal of this book is to help you use writing to discover what you think and feel. "Good writing is clear thinking made visible." (Bill Wheeler, educator)

Revising Writing

The second goal of this book is to convince you that a first draft is just a starting point. Look at the draft from your reader's viewpoint. How can you make it more interesting or easier for the reader to follow? Work with what you have written. Dig deeper into your subject. Look for new ideas. Reviewing your draft and making changes is called **revising.** All good writers learn to revise their work.

Writing with a Partner or with a Group

You may think that writing is something you do on your own. However, parts of the writing process can be much more effective—and much more fun—if you do them with others. Share ideas and details about a topic; ask questions about a piece; evaluate what works and doesn't work; edit together for spelling and punctuation; or create a group product.

When you work with others, give feedback that is helpful rather than discouraging or hurtful. Make comments like these:

- "I especially liked . . ."
- "I'm not sure I understand . . ."
- "I would like to know more about . . ."
- "Maybe you could . . ."

At times, you may wish to work alone. You should always have that option.

Portfolios

Keep your finished writing in a portfolio. Its contents will become a lasting record of your improving writing skills.

Adult Education Success Stories

Each chapter in this book tells the story of an adult student who worked long and hard to create a fulfilling life. Learning to read and write well was an important part of their success stories. These true stories show that success is possible, even under difficult and challenging circumstances.

Now, write! Revise! And may you succeed in reaching your goals, too!

CHAPTER

1

People Who Read, Succeed

Writing Skill:
One Point, One Paragraph

Imagine growing up in a home where no English was spoken. You learned no alphabet, no days of the week, no numbers. When you went to school, everyone seemed to know more than you did. You were very quiet, and you tried to disappear in the large classroom.

When a problem occurred, your mother felt incapable of talking with a teacher or counselor. She pulled you out of school.

This happened year after year after year. By high school, you still couldn't read. Kids teased, you suffered, and your mother took you out of school for good. At home, you cooked, cleaned, and knew you had no future. You were not sure that living was worthwhile.

Then, a miracle occurred, and you discovered a capable, confident self that you never dreamed existed!

Reading. It can make all the difference.

This is Viridiana's story.

"I Can't Believe How My Life Has Changed."

"Viridiana, it's your turn," the tenth-grade English teacher said. "Please read the next page aloud."

Viridiana Ramos tried her best, but she could barely read at all. Laughter **erupted** in the room. Viridiana wanted to disappear under her desk.

She had never finished a whole year of school. Her mother spoke no English and had little education. When Viridiana was being bullied or had another major problem, her mother simply took her out of school. In her family, education was not a **priority.**

The English teacher **recommended** that Viridiana get help from the school's Reading Center. Viridiana went twice, but the secretary just talked on the phone and ignored her. No one helped her. Discouraged, she dropped out of school.

Viridiana was depressed for the next two years. All she did was cook and clean. She wanted to learn to read, to finish high school, and to get a good job.

One day, Viridiana's sister met two tutors from a literacy council. They encouraged her to bring Viridiana to their program. Painfully shy, never raising her eyes, Viridiana went. She tested at the third-grade reading level. More important, she decided to try the program.

Although she was nervous at first, Viridiana loved it! She was the youngest in a class of six. The classmates became friends and helped each other. The staff was kind. And a dedicated tutor named Alice studied with Viridiana two mornings a week.

In a small class where the pace was slow, Viridiana found that she *could* learn. She was an enthusiastic, patient, hardworking student. For seven months, she studied letter sounds and syllables. After that, Viridiana found herself at a new, higher reading level. Exciting new worlds began to open up!

Over the next two years, Viridiana earned 145 credits and received her diploma. She gained great self-confidence, and her life became full of hope and possibilities.

Today, Viridiana Ramos is an area **administrator** for a home-**mortgage** company, a job she loves. She will forever feel grateful to Alice and the adult-school staff for their help and **encouragement.** Learning to read and write well completely **transformed** her life.

Vocabulary

erupted – burst out
priority – something of great importance
recommended – suggested
administrator – person in charge
mortgage – loan against property
encouragement – support
transformed – changed

Vocabulary Exercise

Write the vocabulary word that best fits each sentence. Then read the sentences aloud.

1. To put my son through college, I took out a ____________________ on my house.

   How many years will it take to pay off your ____________________?

   I'll pay off the ____________________ in 20 years.

2. The teachers gave Viridiana a lot of ____________________.

   Most people need ____________________ when they are having a hard time.

   Without ____________________, it is easy to lose hope.

3. A tutor's first ____________________ is to teach reading.

   Suppose the student's ____________________ is math?

   Then, they will have to discuss what their joint ____________________ should be.

4. Viridiana is an ____________________ at a mortgage company.

   An ____________________ has a lot of responsibility.

   Usually, a dedicated employee is chosen to become an ____________________.

5. The students ____________________ in laughter.

   Then, the teacher's laugh ____________________ as well.

   They ____________________ with joy when their team won the game.

6. The teacher ____________________ that Viridiana go to the Reading Center.

   Viridiana did as he ____________________, but she received no help.

   The tutors ____________________ that Viridiana come to their adult program.

7. Success at the adult school ____________________ Viridiana into an outgoing person.

   Learning to read ____________________ her self-image.

   By meeting her goals, she ____________________ her life.

React to the Story

Relax. Then write your thoughts about the story. For five minutes, write whatever comes to mind. Don't worry about details. Just write.

____

____

____

____

____

____

____

____

Writing Skill: One Point, One Paragraph

A paragraph should have only one main idea. The rest of the paragraph should support that one idea with interesting details. When writers move on to new ideas, they start new paragraphs.

Reread the last two paragraphs of Viridiana's story on page 6. In which of them might this sentence belong? "She became friendly and outgoing."

Here are two main ideas:

1. Viridiana's mother did not support her desire for education.
2. Viridiana loved her new school.

**Put a 1 beside each sentence that belongs in a paragraph with the first main idea.
Put a 2 beside each sentence that belongs with the second main idea.**

_____ Her mother wanted her to drop out of adult school and stay home.

_____ It became her home away from home.

_____ For the first time in her life, she felt good about her abilities.

_____ She did not think it was important to graduate.

_____ She began to help out, answering phones and tutoring new students.

_____ No one at home ever tried to help her with her schoolwork.

_____ The students and staff became her good friends.

_____ Her mother felt that she was losing Viridiana to the new school.

Get Ready to Write

Assignment

Write a paragraph about a time when you felt proud of yourself.

Think of a time when you were proud of yourself for something that you accomplished. What was the situation? How did you feel? Why did you feel that way? In the space below, write brief notes about the experience.

Now organize your notes. Circle what seems most important to you. Cross out any ideas that don't seem to fit.

Write

Write the paragraph. This is your first draft.

In each of this book's chapters, you will be asked to review your writing against a **rubric.** Rubrics can help you make effective changes to your writing. A rubric contains features to look for, and it describes how well each feature has been done. When you finish comparing your writing to a rubric, you'll see what needs to be improved.

Reread your paragraph. Then evaluate it against this rubric. *In each row,* circle the box that best describes your paragraph.

Feature	Well Done!	OK	Needs Work
Structure	Paragraph has one main idea. Topic sentence states it.	Paragraph is about one idea. No topic sentence makes it clear.	Paragraph mentions several ideas. No one main idea stands out.
Content	Main idea supported by three or more details. All details directly related to main point.	Paragraph mentions one or two details. Not all details relate to main point.	Paragraph does not include details. Details do not relate to main point.
Organization	Main idea and details are in an order that makes sense.	Idea sequence is a little confusing.	Ideas in no particular order. Hard to understand.

Did you circle statements under *OK* and *Needs Work?* Look under *Well Done!* in the same row to see how to improve your writing.

Revise

First drafts are never perfect. In this book, you will always be asked to revise your work. After considering the rubric, answer these questions.

1. What main idea did you want to express in your paragraph? Write your topic sentence below.

____

____

2. Do the other sentences in your paragraph relate to that main idea? Cross out any sentences that do not.

3. Does your paragraph need more details to support its topic sentence? On your first draft, make a note of any details you want to add.

4. Decide which sentences should come first, second, etc. Show the sequence by writing the numbers 1, 2, 3, etc., before the sentences and ideas in your draft.

5. Now, rewrite your paragraph, following your plan. Put your main idea in a topic sentence; then write sentences using the supporting details that you have chosen in the sequence you like.

It is often helpful to work with one or more other people when reviewing and revising your work. Here are some guidelines for working with others.

- Have the writer read the passage aloud. Listen carefully.
- Look for what is good in the passage. Be specific. ("I especially liked...")
- Locate problems. Again, be specific. ("I'm not sure I understand...")
- Make constructive suggestions. ("Maybe you could...")
- Ask questions. ("Can you tell me more about...?""Why did you...?")
- Avoid discouraging or hurtful remarks. Respond as you hope others will respond to your writing.

6. Share your paragraph with a writing partner. Then evaluate it against this rubric. Notice the new features. Decide together which statement *in each row* best describes your work. Then circle the statements.

Feature	Well Done!	OK	Needs Work
Structure	Paragraph has one main idea. Topic sentence states it.	Paragraph is about one idea. No topic sentence makes it clear.	Paragraph mentions several ideas. No one main idea stands out.
Content	Main idea supported by three or more details. All details directly related to main point.	Paragraph mentions one or two details. Not all details relate to main point.	Paragraph does not include details. Details do not relate to main point.
Organization	Main idea and details are in an order that makes sense.	Idea sequence is a little confusing.	Ideas in no particular order. Hard to understand.
Capitalization	First word in each sentence is capitalized.	Capitalization of initial words is inconsistent.	No capitalization of first words in sentences.
Punctuation	Sentences end with a period, question mark, or exclamation point.	Most sentences end with correct punctuation.	End punctuation is inconsistent or incorrect.

Discuss with your writing partner what you can do to improve your rubric rating.

7. With your partner, edit your paragraph.

Produce and Present

Prepare a final, edited version of your paragraph for your portfolio.

CHAPTER

2

Perseverance

Writing Skill:
Generating Ideas

If anyone had good reason to give up on learning to read and write, it was Richard Evans. By the third grade, he didn't even know the alphabet. Kids were mean. Teachers seemed unable to help, and Richard felt lost and confused. School was a nightmare. He finally quit school just after his 18th birthday. But alcohol and drugs soon took over his life.

A few years later, while being tested for depression, Richard found out that he had several major learning difficulties. He felt encouraged. He wasn't dumb! Maybe there were ways to work around these problems. He knew he would like himself better if he could read and write, so he decided to try formal learning again.

But time after time, he met with failure. Most people would have given up. It was Richard's perseverance, his determination to keep going in spite of setbacks, that enabled him to succeed.

This is Richard's story.

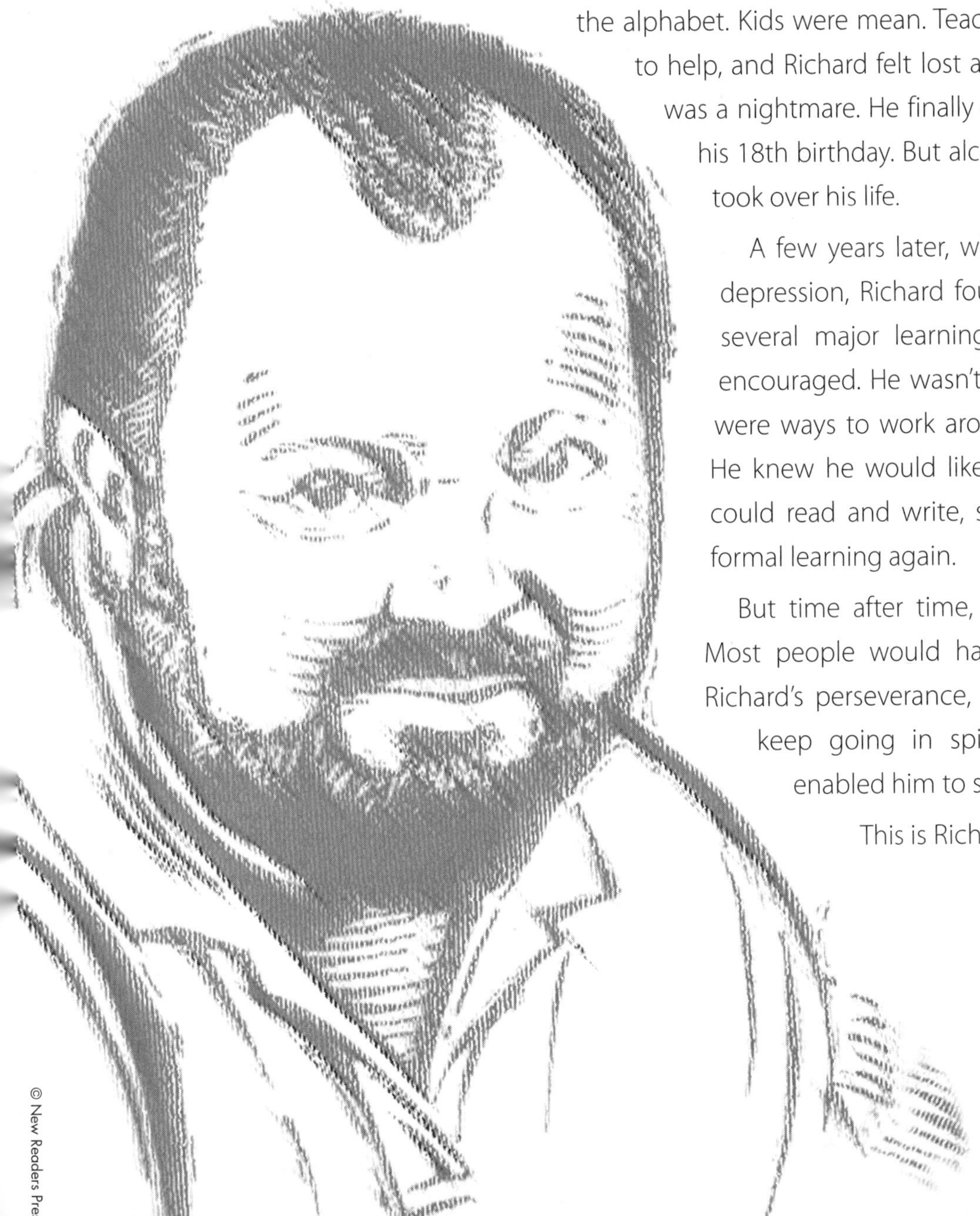

"If I Can Do It, Anyone Can."

By the time he was in junior high, Richard had a **phobia** about school. School was torture. He threw up every morning and had bad dreams every night. During the school day, he tried to make himself **invisible.**

Fortunately, Richard was talented in electronics. When he dropped out of school at 18, he got a good job working with a robotic cutting tool. At last, he felt like a success!

However, his private life was not so successful. He married, but the marriage was not happy. He got involved with alcohol and drugs. Richard began to hate his life.

Then he heard about a book, *Tough Times Never Last, But Tough People Do* by Robert Schuller. With his wife's help, Richard "read" his first book, and it made him want to change his life. He entered a **residential** treatment **facility.**

While in recovery, Richard began to write a journal. Writing was hard for him, but he found that it helped him with his reading. He knew that he might never feel better about himself unless he could read and write well.

Richard decided to enroll in a literacy program. He was told, "You *can* learn, but you have to do it your own way." What a relief. There was hope!

Because he learned differently from others, he couldn't just sit and study one thing at a time. Learning was much easier for him when he had two or three computers going at once, each involving a different project. He also found a reading program for his computer that pronounced words as he read along. Slowly, he made progress.

More confident now, Richard wanted to re-enter school. His first effort to **conquer** his school **phobia** was to drive by the community college many times. Next, he parked for 30-minute periods in the parking lot. At last, he entered the building.

Seeking **nontraditional** students, the college accepted him. But Richard dropped out after three weeks, **overwhelmed.** He studied on his own for a year and then tried again. This time, he succeeded! When he shared his struggles with a speech class, they said, "Richard, you have to share your story with others!" This became the focus of his new life. He majored in special education and now teaches and counsels others with learning differences.

Richard calls his learning differences a gift because they led him to work that he feels passionate about. His life is now spent giving hope to others.

Vocabulary

phobia – crippling fear
invisible – unable to be seen
residential – where people live
facility – a building with a special purpose
conquer – overcome
nontraditional – not customary
overwhelmed – helpless; defeated

Vocabulary Exercise

Write the vocabulary word that best fits each sentence. Then complete the open sentences. Read the sentences aloud.

1. Going back to school ______________ Richard.

   What in life has ______________ you?

   Overwhelmed means ______________________________.

2. Some rehabilitation facilities are open only during the day, but others are ______________.

   Cities have industrial areas and ______________ areas.

   Residential means ______________________________.

3. Some dog fences are ______________. An electric signal is what keeps dogs in the yard.

   Using mirrors, a magician can make himself seem ______________.

   Invisible means ______________________________.

4. His new confidence made him feel that he could ______________ all!

   It takes practice to ______________ the fear of public speaking.

   Conquer means ______________________________.

5. There is a fish-packing ______________ on the other side of town.

   Have you toured the school's new technical ______________?

   Facility means ______________________________.

6. Many people have a ______________ about flying.

   Do you have a ______________ about snakes?

   Phobia means ______________________________.

7. Some schools take a ______________ approach to teaching.

   Many Asian women now wear ______________ dress.

   Nontraditional means ______________________________.

React to the Story

Write about the story. For five minutes, write whatever comes to mind. Don't worry about details. Just write.

Writing Skill: Generating Ideas

Sometimes it is hard to think of ideas to write about. In this chapter, you'll try two of the many ways to come up with ideas for writing: creating an idea web, and talking with someone about your topic.

The diagram below is called an **idea web.** Use it to help you gather and organize your ideas before writing. Write a main idea in the center circle. Then write related ideas or details in the surrounding circles.

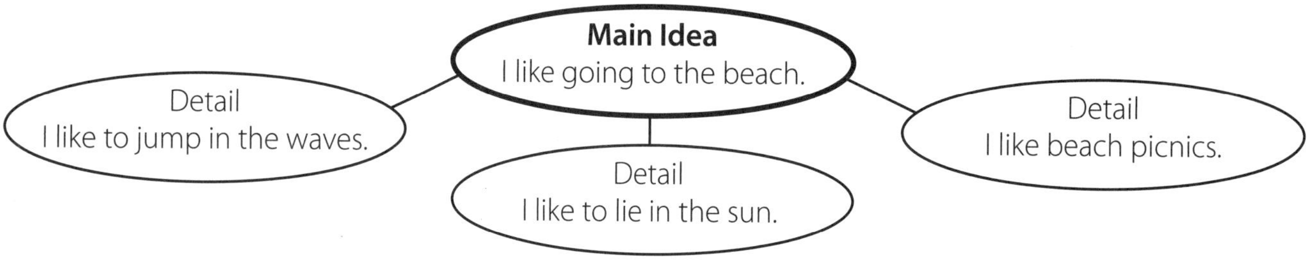

Get Ready to Write

Assignment

Write a paragraph about a problem that someone has and does not want to face.

1. Think about a friend or family member who has a problem that he or she doesn't want to face. Make up a name for that person if you wish. Pick a situation that you are willing to discuss with a classmate or writing partner.

2. Think about the situation. Why is the situation a problem? Does it hurt the person? Does it hurt other people? Why do you think the person is avoiding the problem? What steps could be taken to solve the problem? Write notes about the situation on a separate piece of paper.

3. Discuss your notes with a classmate or writing partner. Ask for helpful comments and questions. Add to your notes, or cross out notes that do not belong on your list.

4. Decide on one main idea for your paragraph. Write that main idea in the center circle of your idea web.

5. Pick two or three supporting ideas, or details, for that main idea. Write the supporting ideas in the other circles in the web.

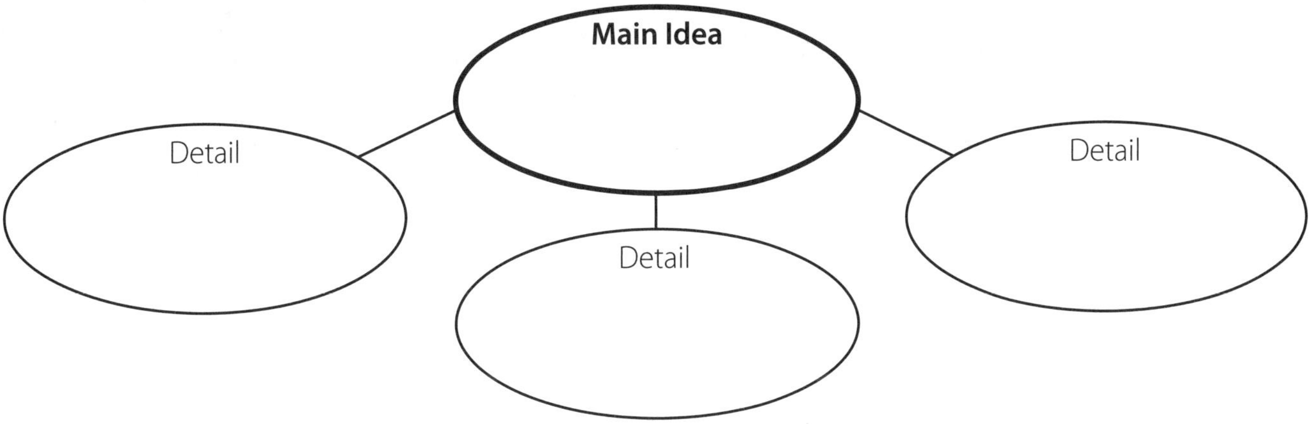

Write

1. Write a paragraph about the person and his or her problem.

2. Reread your paragraph. Then evaluate it against this rubric. *In each row,* circle the statement that best describes your paragraph.

Feature	Well Done!	OK	Needs Work
Structure	Paragraph has one main idea. Topic sentence states it.	Paragraph is about one idea. No topic sentence makes it clear.	Paragraph mentions several ideas. No one main idea stands out.
Content	Main idea supported by three or more details. All details directly related to main point.	Paragraph mentions one or two details. Not all details relate to main point.	Paragraph does not include details. Details do not relate to main point.
Organization	Main idea and details are in an order that makes sense.	Idea sequence is a little confusing.	Ideas in no particular order. Hard to understand.

Did you circle statements under *OK* and *Needs Work?* Look under *Well Done!* in the same row to see how to improve your writing.

Revise

You wrote the first draft for yourself. Now suppose that you want to send the paragraph to the person with the problem. You might make some changes. This is called adapting your writing for a different audience. Always write with your audience in mind.

1. Share your paragraph with a classmate or writing partner. Ask that person to pretend he or she is the person with the problem. Ask, "How does reading what I wrote make you feel? Hurt? Upset? Understood? Hopeless?" Discuss the following ideas:

   - **Tone. Tone** is the overall manner in which words are spoken or written. Is the tone accusing? Sympathetic? Encouraging?

   - **Word choice.** Which words set the tone of the writing? Do the words say precisely what you mean?

2. Discuss any changes you would make before writing to the person with the problem. What tone would you aim for? What words would help achieve that tone?

3. Make notes on your first draft about these changes.

4. Revise your paragraph. Write it to the person who has the problem.

- Choose your words carefully.
- Keep the person in mind while you write. Write directly to that person.
- Put the most important idea first, then follow with supporting ideas.

5. If possible, work with a writing partner. Otherwise, think by yourself about what you learned in this chapter. Consider these questions:

   - What did you like or dislike about using the idea web?
   - Did talking with others help you think of more ideas?
   - How did having a specific reader in mind change your writing?

6. Share your paragraph with your writing partner. Then evaluate it against this rubric. Decide together which statement *in each row* best describes your work. Then circle the statements.

Feature	Well Done!	OK	Needs Work
Audience	Paragraph written directly to its audience.	Audience is not clear.	No apparent attempt to write to a specific audience.
Structure	Paragraph has one main idea. Topic sentence states it.	Paragraph is about one idea. No topic sentence makes it clear.	Paragraph mentions several ideas. No one main idea stands out.
Content	Main idea supported by three or more details. All details directly related to main point.	Paragraph mentions one or two details. Not all details relate to main point.	Paragraph does not include details. Details do not relate to main point.
Organization	Main idea and details are in an order that makes sense.	Idea sequence is a little confusing.	Ideas in no particular order. Hard to understand.
Word Choice	Tone and word choice fit audience well.	Some attempt to choose words and tone to fit audience.	Tone and word choice not tailored for audience.

Discuss with your writing partner what you can do to improve your writing.

7. Review the Editing Checklist on page 93. A checklist is helpful when you are nearly done with a piece of writing. Use it as a guide when you make your final edits.

   Edit your revised paragraph. Pay particular attention to the first five points on the Editing Checklist.

Produce and Present

Prepare a final, edited version of your paragraph to keep in your portfolio.

CHAPTER

3

Beating the Odds

Writing Skill:
Adjusting for Audience

Jason Donaldson had a very rough childhood. The odds were slim that he would be able to build a life of his own choosing. Yet, at 33, Jason is training to be a chef, the occupation of his dreams.

A small part of his success was luck. He was never in the wrong place at the wrong time. But a larger success was the result of making good decisions. He steered clear of the hard drugs that destroyed many lives in his neighborhood. And he enrolled in GED classes to work on math and writing, in spite of his fears.

Most of all, Jason succeeded because he steadily avoided the negative influences in life. He purposely looked for the positive things that would lead him toward the life he wanted.

Steady movement along the right road enabled Jason to beat the odds.

This is Jason's story.

"I'm Lucky Just to Be Here."

Earning a GED was an important **milestone** in Jason Donaldson's life, but his diploma was only one important result of his recent classes. "I discovered I was more **capable** than I thought," Jason says. "For the first time in my life, I began to feel good about myself."

Self-esteem and self-confidence are remarkable characteristics in a man with Jason's background. His father died when he was two. Low income forced Jason and his mother to live in an apartment on the **notorious** south side of Chicago. "The housing projects across the street were depressing places, filled with drugs, guns, and hopelessness. Everyone felt stuck. Generations of families were just existing, not really living." Jason is grateful to have survived life in his neighborhood. "I'm lucky just to be here."

School was no escape. Small for his age, Jason was constantly picked on. By the third grade, he was skipping school. He spent his days touring Chicago, "learning more than I could have in class." Luckily, he became a good reader at an early age. "I learned that if a story or book was written right, you saw images, not words." When Jason dropped out of school in the 11th grade, he was doing well in every subject except math.

For several years, he worked at a pizza shop. Later, he became an activity aide at a nursing home. When that job was **downsized,** he wanted to find similar work. But he realized that he would need a diploma or a GED to get a good job. He had thought about going back to school before, but fear had made him **procrastinate.** This time, he felt he had no choice.

It was the best thing that could have happened. Jason went to class four nights every week to work on his math and writing skills. Soon, he was ready to take the GED test, but there was a four-month waiting list. He continued attending classes and then passed the test with honors!

Jason had always enjoyed cooking. With encouragement from his teachers, he entered a **culinary** school. He earns As and Bs and even takes time to **mentor** several of the younger students. Now, Jason loves being a student chef and using his artistic skills to design attractive food presentations.

Vocabulary

milestone – important step toward a goal
capable – able to do things well
notorious – famous for negative reasons
downsized – cut to save the employer money
procrastinate – keep putting off; delay
culinary – related to cooking
mentor – teach; coach; advise; guide

Vocabulary Exercise

Write the vocabulary word that best fits each sentence. Then complete the open sentences. Read the sentences aloud.

1. My son should do his report today, but I know he will ____________________.

   If you ____________________, you will miss the deadline.

   I procrastinate when ____.

2. Did you hear the news? Chris got a scholarship to study ____________________ arts.

   Lisa won one of the ____________________ prizes at the fair.

   Culinary means ____.

3. Getting a GED is an important ____________________ in many people's lives.

   Beginning kindergarten is a real ____________________ for children.

   ____ was a milestone in my life.

4. Hitler was ____________________ for his cruelty.

   That restaurant is ____________________ for its slow service.

   The notorious thief ____.

5. Jobs at the shop were ____________________ because fewer orders were coming in.

   When his job was ____________________, he qualified for unemployment.

   If my job were downsized, ____.

6. Many adults volunteer to ____________________ troubled youths.

   Jason took time to ____________________ some of the younger students.

   To mentor is to ____.

7. Jason knows that he is much more____________________ than he used to think he was.

   Chris is a very ____________________ basketball player.

   I know I am capable when ____.

React to the Story

Write about the story. For five minutes, write whatever comes to mind. Don't worry about details. Just write.

Writing Skill: Adjusting for Audience

We use informal language when we talk with friends or relatives. When you write to people you know well, you usually write informally, too. When you read it aloud, informal writing sounds as if you are speaking. It may include slang and casual expressions, and it has a conversational tone.

Writing to public officials and businesses requires a different, more formal tone. Businesspeople prefer letters that come right to the point. They want all the information they need, but nothing more. And they expect to read proper English, correctly spelled and well presented. To accomplish your goals, use formal writing when you conduct business.

When you write, think first about your reader. Would it be better to write formally or informally to that reader?

Which of the following passages would belong in a formal letter?

> "Poor old Mrs. Benson. Dragging those grocery bags up 13 flights of stairs is going to be the death of her. And there's Sam in his wheelchair! No way he can get to another floor when the elevator's not working."

> "Many of our residents are elderly. Those with serious physical problems may find climbing many flights of stairs difficult, especially if they are carrying heavy loads. We also have disabled and wheelchair-bound residents. Without a working elevator, they are not able to leave their floors."

Reread Jason's story. Does it use formal or informal writing?

Get Ready to Write

Assignment

Invite neighbors to a meeting about a neighborhood problem.
Then write a formal complaint to a government office.

1. Pretend you are Jason. The elevator in your tall building is often broken. This creates many problems for you and your neighbors. Create an informal flyer about the elevator situation. Or choose another community issue that is important to you and your neighbors. In the flyer, invite the neighbors to a meeting to seek a solution. Include at least three reasons why you think that this is a serious problem. You will need more than one paragraph. Make sure each paragraph is about just one main idea.

Brainstorming is another way of getting ideas for writing. You can brainstorm alone, but the technique works better with two or more people.

- Write the topic.
- As quickly as possible, list every idea or word about that topic that comes into your head. Don't stop to think, just list ideas as fast as you can.
- After a few minutes, stop. Review your list. Which ideas do you like best? Organize and expand those ideas. Discard the rest.

2. Brainstorm with a writing partner about the situation. What problems would it cause? Write your ideas below.

____

____

3. Decide what you want to say in your flyer. Describe the problem, and then invite your neighbors to the meeting.

Main idea ______________________________________

Detail ______________________________________

Detail ______________________________________

Detail ______________________________________

Main idea ______________________________________

Detail ______________________________________

Detail ______________________________________

Write

Write your flyer on the lines below. Indent the first line of each new paragraph.

Revise

Reread your flyer. Did you use informal language when you wrote to the neighbors? Which words or phrases show informality?

Assume that your group decided at the meeting to make an official complaint. Change your informal flyer into a formal letter of complaint.

1. Plan what you will write.

Beginning:

Tell why you are writing.	Purpose:

Middle:

Explain the issue.	Main idea (problem): Reason: Reason: Reason:

End:

Request a specific action.	Action requested:
Thank the reader.	Closing:

2. Address your letter to the government official in your area who deals with your kind of complaint. For example, Jason would write to his local housing authority. Your teacher or a librarian can help you find the right person.

3. Write your letter on a separate piece of paper. Type it if you can.

   - Put your name, address, and the date at the top of the page.
   - Then write the name, title, and address of the official.
   - Greet the official (for example, "Dear Commissioner Carter:").
   - Write your letter. Indent and start a new paragraph when you move to a new main idea.
   - Use transition words like "first," "in addition," "as a result," and "for example." These show relationships between your sentences. They can help readers to follow the sequence of your ideas.
   - Close the letter with "Sincerely," and your name.

   Write clearly and convincingly. Use formal language. Be firm, but not angry.

4. Work with a writing partner to evaluate your letter against this rubric. Decide together which statement *in each row* best describes your letter. Circle the statements.

Feature	Well Done!	OK	Needs Work
Purpose/ Audience	Letter's purpose is clearly stated right at the beginning. Letter is written directly to its audience.	The purpose is stated, but not at the beginning. Letter seems to shift audience from one part to another.	Letter's purpose is not stated. No apparent attempt to write to a specific audience.
Structure	Letter ends with clear request for a specific action.	A request for action is present, but it is not specific.	No request for action in the letter.
Content	All details in body of letter support its purpose.	Some unimportant or unrelated details included.	Letter includes many unrelated, unimportant details.
Organization	Ideas are in logical, convincing order. Transition words show relationships between sentences.	Idea sequence is a little confusing. Occasional transition words.	Ideas in no particular order. No transition words. Relationships between sentences unclear and confusing.
Word Choice	Levels of formality and politeness fit the audience well.	Inconsistent levels of formality and politeness.	Levels of formality and politeness do not fit audience.

Did you circle statements under *OK* and *Needs Work?* Look under *Well Done!* in the same row to see how to improve your writing.

Produce and Present

Review the checklist on page 93. Make any needed final edits. Be especially careful when editing business letters if you want to be taken seriously.

Prepare a final copy of your letter to keep in your portfolio.

If you wrote about your own issue, consider sending your letter to the government official you identified.

CHAPTER

4

Forge Your Own Path

Writing Skill:
Questioning

In this story, an admissions counselor put a roadblock in Cynthia's pathway to college. Many people in her situation might have become discouraged and given up. But because Cynthia relied on her own judgment and initiative, she was able to pursue her dream.

Some people seem to be born with the ability to make their own way. Others learn the skill later in life, and still others never seem to get the knack. It is clear, though, that people who pay attention to their own thoughts and judgments are more likely to lead lives that are pleasing to them than are the people who depend on others for their opinions and actions.

This is Cynthia's story.

"You're Wrong About Me!"

Confused, Cynthia Brooks stared at the dots and words on the college admissions test. The counselor called them **analogies.** She'd never seen a test like this one before. How could analogies tell the university whether she would do well at their school?

Panic grabbed her; she couldn't think. **Precious** seconds slipped away, taking her dreams of college with them. Thirty minutes later, she looked at her awful test results.

"I'm sorry," said the counselor, "but our test shows that you're not quite ready for college-level work. Why don't you study for another year? Then, come back and see us."

Cynthia walked out of the building on shaky legs. Come back in a year? No way! She would never **humiliate** herself like that again. The words she'd heard all her life replayed in her head. *You're stupid. You'll never amount to anything. You need to learn your place.* She closed her eyes, as she waited at the bus stop, longing for the privacy of home.

For days, Cynthia kept busy and tried to forget the **incident.** Then she remembered that writing had helped her cope with problems in the past. She dug out her old journal and **browsed** through it. She **winced** at the **anguished** thoughts that she'd recorded during arguments with her often-absent mom and during the time when she had lost custody of her son.

Cynthia updated the journal: she'd earned her GED, which hadn't been as hard as she'd feared. She'd grown confident in her abilities and felt sure that she could do well in college.

It was that test! The thought made her sit upright. *If they had given me the kind of test that I'm used to taking, I'd have done a lot better. Do all admissions offices use that kind of test?* She tossed the journal aside and picked up the phone book. She was going to find out.

Two weeks later, Cynthia glowed with satisfaction as she left a different admissions office. She had not only passed their test and been accepted, but she had qualified for 100 percent financial aid as well!

She wondered how many other people's plans had been frustrated by their results on that test. She was glad that she had paid attention to her own thoughts, instead of accepting the counselor's judgment.

Vocabulary

analogies – test questions that compare relationships among words

precious – of great value

humiliate – shame or embarrass

incident – brief, unplanned event

browsed – skimmed; looked over casually

winced – made a brief movement in pain

anguished – filled with pain

Vocabulary Exercise

Write the vocabulary word that best fits each sentence. Then read the sentences aloud.

1. Cynthia didn't want to ____________________ herself by going there again.

   The bullies liked to ____________________ the younger boys.

   Forcing students to read out loud may ____________________ them.

2. She ____________________ through the college catalog while she waited.

   Many people ____________________ through items offered at the garage sale.

   I ____________________ through the magazines in the library until it closed.

3. Her ____________________ thoughts kept her tossing and turning all night.

   The puppy let out ____________________ cries when her owner left the house.

   It's hard to watch the ____________________ faces of the family at a funeral.

4. Cynthia was going to study ____________________ just to prove she could do them.

   ____________________ ask you to compare word meanings.

   The GED uses no ____________________, but college admission tests may include them.

5. Cynthia tried to forget the ____________________ in the counselor's office.

   That ____________________ in the parking lot made us all late.

   Were you there when the lunchroom ____________________ erupted?

6. The runner ____________________ when she sprained her ankle.

   She ____________________ at the cost of the car repairs.

   Rafael ____________________ when he got his tetanus shot.

7. Photographs from long ago can be very ____________________.

   Is anything more ____________________ than a baby's first smile?

   To someone who has survived serious illness, every day is ____________________.

React to the Story

Write about the story. For five minutes, write whatever comes to mind. Don't worry about details. Just write.

Writing Skill: Questioning

Rarely do writers' best ideas appear in their first drafts. The brain seems to need to warm up before it can generate its best thoughts. So don't stop the process after finishing your first draft; your most important thoughts might be just beginning to rise to the surface.

One way you can uncover hidden ideas is by questioning. Once you have finished a first draft, go back through it and think of questions you would like to ask the subject of the story, such as "Why did you do that?" or "If the same thing happened today, would you react in the same way?"

For instance, after reading Cynthia's story, you might want an answer to this question:

How did your mom's frequent absences affect you?

1. Reread Cynthia's story. With a writing partner, think of questions you would like to ask Cynthia. What information is left out? What else would you like to know?
2. Gather all the questions that the members of your group or class came up with. Then think about how you might include some of that additional information in Cynthia's story. This questioning strategy is a great way to identify details that would make your writing more interesting to a reader.

Get Ready to Write

Assignment

Write a story for a young friend or relative. Tell about a specific time when someone you know succeeded at a task by relying on his or her own judgment.

1. With a writing partner, brainstorm situations you might write about. In the space below, write a few words that will help you remember each idea.

____

____

____

2. Choose the one situation that you would most like to share. Write your main ideas and some supporting thoughts. Then organize these notes. What will you write about first? Second? Number the ideas in order. Plan to start a new paragraph whenever you change to a new main idea.

Main idea ________________________________

Detail ________________________________

Detail ________________________________

Detail ________________________________

Main idea ________________________________

Detail ________________________________

Detail ________________________________

Detail ________________________________

Main idea ________________________________

Detail ________________________________

Detail ________________________________

Detail ________________________________

Write

On a separate piece of paper, write your story. In your mind, picture the young person to whom you are writing. Remember to indent each paragraph.

Revise

Try the questioning technique with the story you just wrote.

1. Read your story to a writing partner or group.
2. Ask listeners to pretend that they are going to interview the subject of your story. Ask them to make lists of questions they would like to ask. If you are working alone, make your own list of questions.
3. Share and discuss the lists. How do you think your subject would answer the questions?
4. In the boxes below, write a few of the questions that interest you most. Then make notes about how you think your subject might answer.

Question	Possible Answer
1	1
2	2
3	3

5. Plan how you will add this new information to your story.

6. Rewrite your story. Make it more interesting by adding the new details that you gathered by using the questioning technique.

Did brainstorming help you come up with ideas for writing?

Did the questioning technique help you think of interesting details to add to you story?

Work with a writing partner to evaluate your story against the rubric below. Decide together which statement *in each row* best describes your story. Circle the statements.

Feature	Well Done!	OK	Needs Work
Audience	Story is written to appeal to its audience.	Not clear for which audience the story is written.	Story is inappropriate for its audience.
Structure	Every main idea has its own paragraph.	Some paragraphs contain more than one main idea.	No clear main ideas in paragraphs.
Content	Story full of interesting and relevant details, reasons, and examples.	Many details, but some are unimportant or unrelated.	Few details; those it has are often unrelated or unimportant.
Organization	Story moves smoothly from a clear beginning to an engaging middle to a satisfying end.	Story seems unfocused, and direction is inconsistent.	Story does not seem to go anywhere.
Word Choice	The story uses specific nouns and verbs and colorful adjectives.	The story uses common, general, and less interesting words.	Vague, overused words make the story seem boring.

Did you circle statements under *OK* and *Needs Work?* Look under *Well Done!* in the same row to see how to improve your writing.

Produce and Present

First, edit your story, using the checklist on page 93. Then prepare a final copy to keep in your portfolio.

Stories are fun to share. Here are some ideas:

- Have a storytelling session. Tell your story to the group, and listen to the stories that your classmates have written.
- Invite an audience to the storytelling session and make it an event!
- Compile the stories into a class book. Make copies for everyone.
- Make a bulletin board display of the stories. Illustrate stories with drawings or photos.

CHAPTER

5

Seek Every Opportunity

Writing Skill:
Interesting Openings

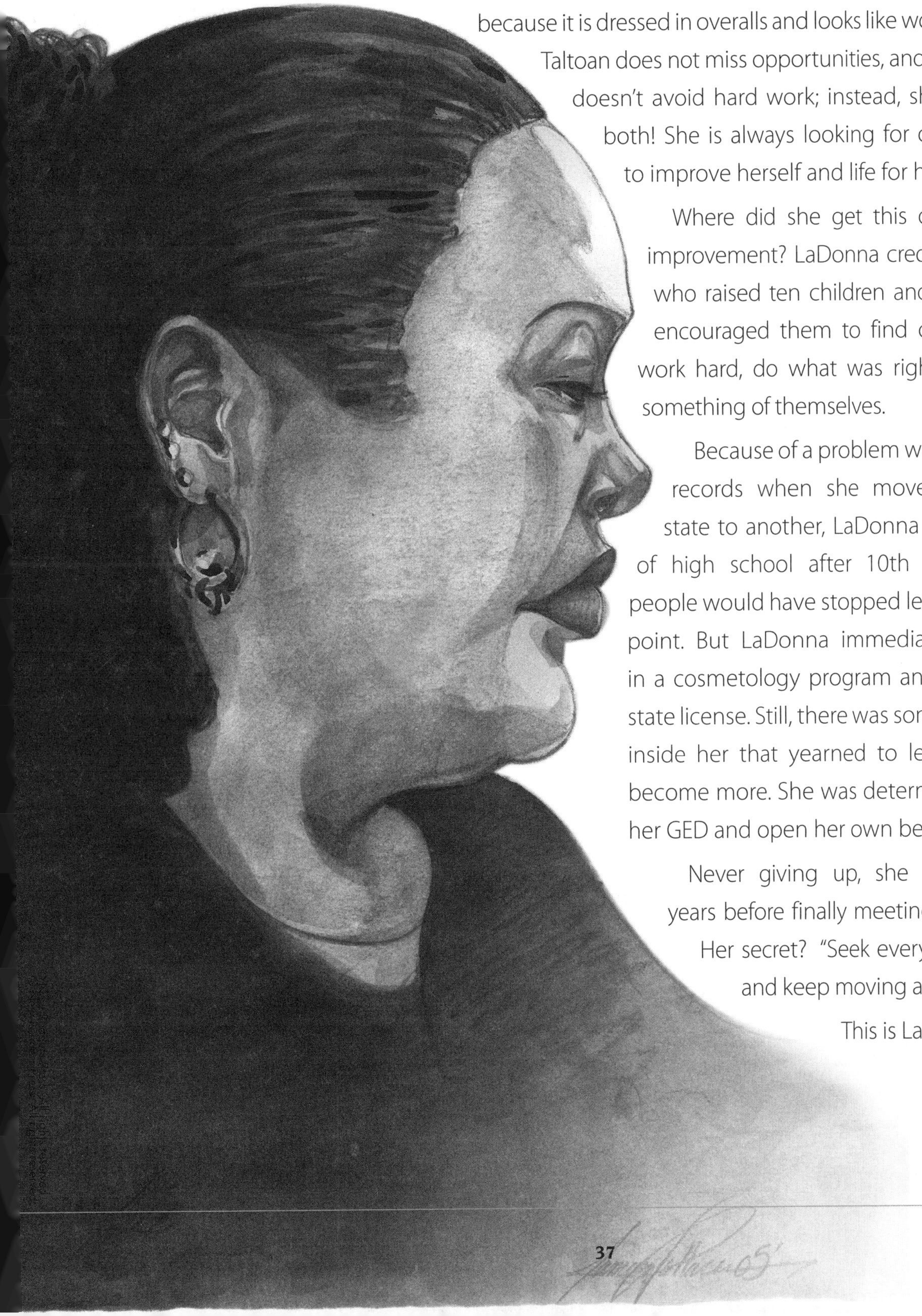

Thomas Edison once said, "Opportunity is missed by most people because it is dressed in overalls and looks like work." LaDonna Taltoan does not miss opportunities, and she certainly doesn't avoid hard work; instead, she thrives on both! She is always looking for opportunities to improve herself and life for her family.

Where did she get this drive for self-improvement? LaDonna credits her mom, who raised ten children and consistently encouraged them to find opportunities, work hard, do what was right, and make something of themselves.

Because of a problem with her school records when she moved from one state to another, LaDonna dropped out of high school after 10th grade. Many people would have stopped learning at that point. But LaDonna immediately enrolled in a cosmetology program and earned her state license. Still, there was something deep inside her that yearned to learn more, to become more. She was determined to earn her GED and open her own beauty shop.

Never giving up, she struggled for years before finally meeting these goals. Her secret? "Seek every opportunity, and keep moving ahead."

This is LaDonna's story.

"Take Advantage of Every Opportunity."

Over the years, LaDonna tried several GED programs without success. Something always got in the way. Tragically, her fiancé was killed, leaving her as the single parent of their infant son. Overwhelmed by her circumstances, LaDonna dropped her studies and struggled daily just to keep going.

The next year, LaDonna met Robert, who would become her husband. Soon, they had a daughter. Since they both worked full-time, LaDonna had trouble attending her evening GED classes and her tutoring sessions in **accounting,** a skill she would need if she were ever to open her own beauty shop. Her first GED practice test score was 187, which was **discouraging** because 225 was the passing score. Still, she attended when she could. Then, the birth of twins put an end to even thinking about studying.

But one day, opportunity knocked on LaDonna's door. A sweet-faced woman said, "Hi, I'm Trish Link from the local literacy program. We offer adult-education classes, day care, and a **certified** preschool, too. That way, whole families can study together. May I tell you about our programs?"

LaDonna smiled. She threw open the door. "Come on in!"

LaDonna started **immediately.** She worked hard and made slow but steady progress.

Soon, she took advantage of another opportunity: a nursing-assistant's class. A few weeks later, LaDonna had a new job as a **Certified** Nursing Assistant. She worked from 11:00 p.m. to 7:00 a.m. She got home just in time to get the older children off to school, and the others ready to go to school with her. It was **exhausting,** but Robert and Trish kept encouraging her. LaDonna was excited about the future.

After five years of study, LaDonna became the proud **recipient** of her GED and was the top student in her class. She and Robert bought a home, and LaDonna opened her own beauty shop. She is doing home-health nursing on weekends, until her **clientele** expands enough to keep the shop open full-time.

LaDonna's future dream? Continue learning by going to college and majoring in communication and religion. She wants to help others make something of their lives, the way so many people have helped her.

Vocabulary

accounting – keeping track of business finances

discouraging – confidence reducing; depressing

certified – officially approved

immediately – right away; without delay

exhausting – very tiring

recipient – a person who gets something

clientele – all of a business's customers together

Vocabulary Exercise

Write a full sentence to answer each question. Use the vocabulary word that fits best in each sentence. Then read the sentence aloud.

1. Working, going to school, and taking care of her family all at the same time was very tiring for LaDonna. What did LaDonna think of her busy life?

____

2. Sam decided to call the adviser right away. When did he decide to call?

____

3. Many people take their taxes to an official accountant. What kind of accountant do they use?

____

4. The one who wins the award will be given a free trip to the Bahamas. Who will get the free trip?

____

5. William's job is keeping track of company finances. In which company department does he probably work?

____

6. At prom time, the hairdresser's number of customers almost doubles. What increases during prom time?

____

7. Job hunters may get depressed as they look for jobs day after day. How would they probably describe the experience to others?

____

React to the Story

Write about the story. For five minutes, write whatever comes to mind. Don't worry about details. Just write.

Writing Skill: Interesting Openings

Reread the opening on page 37. It begins with a quote that might make readers smile and attract their interest.

Now reread the first paragraph of LaDonna's story on page 38. It begins with a problem. The reader might want to see how the problem is solved.

Another good opening for LaDonna's story might have been the disappointing moment when she read her initial practice test score of 187. A reader might want to find out how she was able to succeed.

An interesting opening grabs attention and makes readers want to keep reading.

Get Ready to Write

A public tribute is a brief essay of appreciation intended for a wide audience. It might be delivered as a speech, or it might be printed in a newsletter or other publication.

Assignment

Think of someone like LaDonna, someone you know and admire who seeks opportunities and works hard to take advantage of them. Write a public tribute to this person, at least two or three paragraphs long, describing what he or she has done to earn your respect and affection. Persuade your reader to appreciate your subject, too.

1. Brainstorm for five minutes about your subject. What do you admire about this person? Let your thoughts flow without editing them. As fast as you can, write words that will remind you of your thoughts. Don't try to write everything; just write a few reminder words.

____

____

____

____

____

____

____

____

2. Organize your thoughts into two or three paragraphs. Think of specific examples and details to support each main idea.

Paragraph 1 Main idea ______________________________

Detail ______________________________

Detail ______________________________

Detail ______________________________

Paragraph 2 Main idea ______________________________

Detail ______________________________

Detail ______________________________

Detail ______________________________

Paragraph 3 Main idea ______________________________

Detail ______________________________

Detail ______________________________

Detail ______________________________

Write

1. Write the first draft of your tribute on a separate piece of paper.

2. Reread your tribute. Then evaluate it against this rubric. *In each row,* circle the statement that best describes your tribute.

Feature	Well Done!	OK	Needs Work
Purpose	Writer's admiration shines through.	Writer describes rather than gives reasons for writing a tribute.	Writer shows lack of interest in person to whom tribute is made.
Structure	Every main idea has its own paragraph and topic sentence. Writer immediately catches reader's attention with an interesting opening sentence.	Some paragraphs contain more than one main idea. Writer has tried to make the opening interesting, but it doesn't work well.	No clear main ideas in paragraphs. Opening is ordinary, and does not draw in readers/ listeners.
Content	Tribute is well-focused and full of interesting and relevant reasons, details, and examples.	Focus is fuzzy. Many details, but some seem unrelated. Few reasons.	Tribute is confusing and hard to follow.
Organization	Ideas flow smoothly from one to the next.	Idea sequence is OK, but ideas don't flow.	Tribute is confusing and hard to follow.

Did you circle statements under *OK* and *Needs Work?* Look under *Well Done!* in the same row to see how to improve your writing.

Revise

1. Pair up with a writing partner and read your tributes out loud.
2. Have your partner ask you at least three questions about the person in your tribute. Use the questions to help you think of interesting details to add. Take notes on the lines below. Then ask your partner questions about his or her tribute.
3. Reread the openings to your tributes. With your partner, think of more dramatic or interesting ways to begin. Add these ideas to your notes.
4. With your partner, review your tribute against the rubric above. Write notes about changes you would like to make.

____

____

____

____

____

____

5. Rewrite your tribute. Include new ideas that surfaced using the questioning technique. Add your new opening.

When you were revising your draft, did the questioning technique help you to think of new details and reasons?

Work with a writing partner to evaluate your tribute against this rubric. *In each row,* circle the statement that best describes your tribute.

Feature	Well Done!	OK	Needs Work
Purpose	Writer's admiration shines through.	Writer describes rather than gives reasons for writing a tribute.	Writer shows lack of interest in person to whom tribute is made.
Structure	Every main idea has its own paragraph and topic sentence. Writer immediately catches reader's attention with an interesting opening sentence.	Some paragraphs contain more than one main idea. Writer has tried to make the opening interesting, but it doesn't work well.	Ideas are jumbled into paragraphs. Opening is ordinary, and does not draw in readers/listeners.
Content	Tribute is well focused and full of interesting and relevant reasons, details, and examples.	Focus is fuzzy. Many details, but some seem unrelated. Few reasons.	No focus. The tribute includes few details or reasons.
Organization	Ideas flow smoothly from one to the next.	Idea sequence is OK, but ideas don't flow.	Tribute is confusing and hard to follow.
Revision	New information fits well into the narrative flow.	New ideas have been added, but they aren't combined well with the earlier draft.	Very little change from original draft.

With your writing partner, discuss what you could do to improve your writing.

Produce and Present

Edit your tribute, using the checklist on page 93. Then prepare a final copy to keep in your portfolio.

Present your tribute:

- When your subject is with you, read the tribute to him or her.
- Send a copy of the tribute to the subject.
- At a gathering that includes the subject, read your tribute aloud.
- Find or take a picture of your subject. Then in a class display, include the picture with a copy of your tribute.
- Add your tribute to a class book or web page.

CHAPTER

6

Go Forward, Despite the Risk

Writing Skill:
Adding Details Using the Five Ws

Arlene Cianelli had to decide whether to borrow thousands of dollars to go to college. She had hoped to help her family escape a life of poverty. But when she was asked to sign the loan form, the sum of money seemed huge! If she borrowed the money and failed to graduate, her family would be in much worse financial condition. The thought frightened her. Should she take the risk?

At some point, most people face decisions that involve risk. Sometimes it helps to discuss a difficult decision with a trusted friend or counselor. Just describing the situation to someone else can clarify it for the speaker. But in the end, decisions come down to whether the possible benefit is worth the risk. Remember, opportunities often present themselves as risks.

This is Arlene's story.

"I Don't Know If I Can Do This!"

Arlene stared at the figure on the bank loan form. To her, it was an overwhelming amount of money. Should she sign the bank note? Signing would commit her and her husband to repaying what could become a lifetime debt.

Arlene was raised in a **blue-collar** coal-mining town near Pittsburgh, PA. At 15, she dropped out of high school to get married. The girls she knew married right after high-school graduation, but she hadn't seen any reason to wait that long. After all, she was mature for her age. She had been taking care of her three younger **siblings** for years, while her parents worked.

Arlene soon learned the value of the education she'd given up so easily. Without a diploma, she was stuck in minimum-wage work. Despite her husband's job and her part-time position, making ends meet was impossible. She could afford to feed her children only meatless spaghetti and scrambled eggs. The family's clothes were worn out from long and hard use. Arlene dreamed of escaping **poverty.** She wanted a better life for her children.

So she came up with a plan: she would earn a GED, get a two-year degree in business, and become a bank teller. Family-friendly hours, decent pay, and good benefits attracted her to this occupation.

Arlene met her first goal of getting her GED. But to go to college she would have to borrow money. She was 23. Would she be able to compete for grades against younger high-school graduates? The loan would have to be repaid even if she failed. Her finances could become worse than they already were.

Something her son's school counselor said kept running through Arlene's mind: "Education is the best **investment** you can make. You're investing in yourself, your future, and your family's future." Borrowing money was the only path Arlene could see out of poverty. It was a risk, a big risk, but one she felt she had to take. She signed on the line labeled **"Debtor."**

Arlene completed her two-year business program, but she didn't stop there. Her goals expanded, and she went on to finish a four-year business degree!

Arlene Cianelli is now the technology coordinator for a large literacy council. She helps adults earn GEDs and become comfortable with computers. As a GED graduate herself, Arlene has great **credibility** with her students. The delayed education that she once considered a **liability** has become a great **asset.**

Vocabulary

blue-collar – describes work, often manual, that requires work clothes

siblings – brothers and sisters

poverty – the state of being poor

investment – money or time spent in hope that it may pay off in the future

debtor – a person who borrows money and must pay it back

credibility – believability; acceptance as being honest or true

liability – disadvantage or barrier

asset – something positive that has value

Vocabulary Exercise

Write the vocabulary word that best fits each sentence. Then complete the open sentences. Read the sentences aloud.

1. People who didn't pay their bills used to be sent to ____________________'s prisons.

   His first experience as a ____________________ came when he bought a new car.

   A debtor is ____.

2. ____________________ workers used to wear blue work shirts.

   White-collar workers have office jobs, while ____________________ workers do physical work.

   Blue-collar means ____.

3. Much of the world's population lives in ____________________.

   Families below the ____________________ line struggle to make ends meet.

   Poverty is ____.

4. Reading to your children every day is an ____________________ in education.

   If you had extra money, would you make an ____________________ in stocks and bonds?

   An investment is ____.

5. Lack of a high-school diploma is a ____________________ for job hunters.

   Sophia's mother spoke very little English. That was her biggest ____________________.

   A liability is ____.

6. The woman and her 12 ____________________ lived in a two-room cabin.

   A middle child has at least one older and at least one younger ____________________.

   A sibling is ____.

7. A good education is a great ____________________.

   Caring deeply for others is an ____________________ for nurses.

   An asset is ____.

8. Arlene's past struggles gave her great ____________________ with her students.

   Mike's vague answers to our questions did not give ____________________ to his story.

   Credibility is ____.

React to the Story

Write about the story. For five minutes, write whatever comes to mind. Don't worry about details. Just write.

Writing Skill: Adding Details Using the Five Ws

In Chapter 4, you used questions to help you think of interesting details to add to your writing. In this chapter, you'll focus that questioning strategy more tightly. Newspaper reporters call these questions the "five Ws": Who? What? When? Where? Why? (and sometimes, How?). Reporters use the five Ws to collect details for their stories.

Get Ready to Write

Assignment

Write a letter to a friend or mentor. Inform your reader about a risky decision that you or someone you know well has made.

1. For five minutes, brainstorm a list of difficult or risky decisions that have been made by you or someone you know well. Write the ideas below as fast as you can think of them.

2. Pick an interesting idea that you are willing to share. Write one sentence describing the decision that was made and why it seems risky to you.

3. In the columns below, list your reasons for and against the decision.

For	**Against**
______________________	______________________
______________________	______________________
______________________	______________________
______________________	______________________
______________________	______________________

4. How could you organize two or three paragraphs about this decision? Complete an idea web to plan your letter.

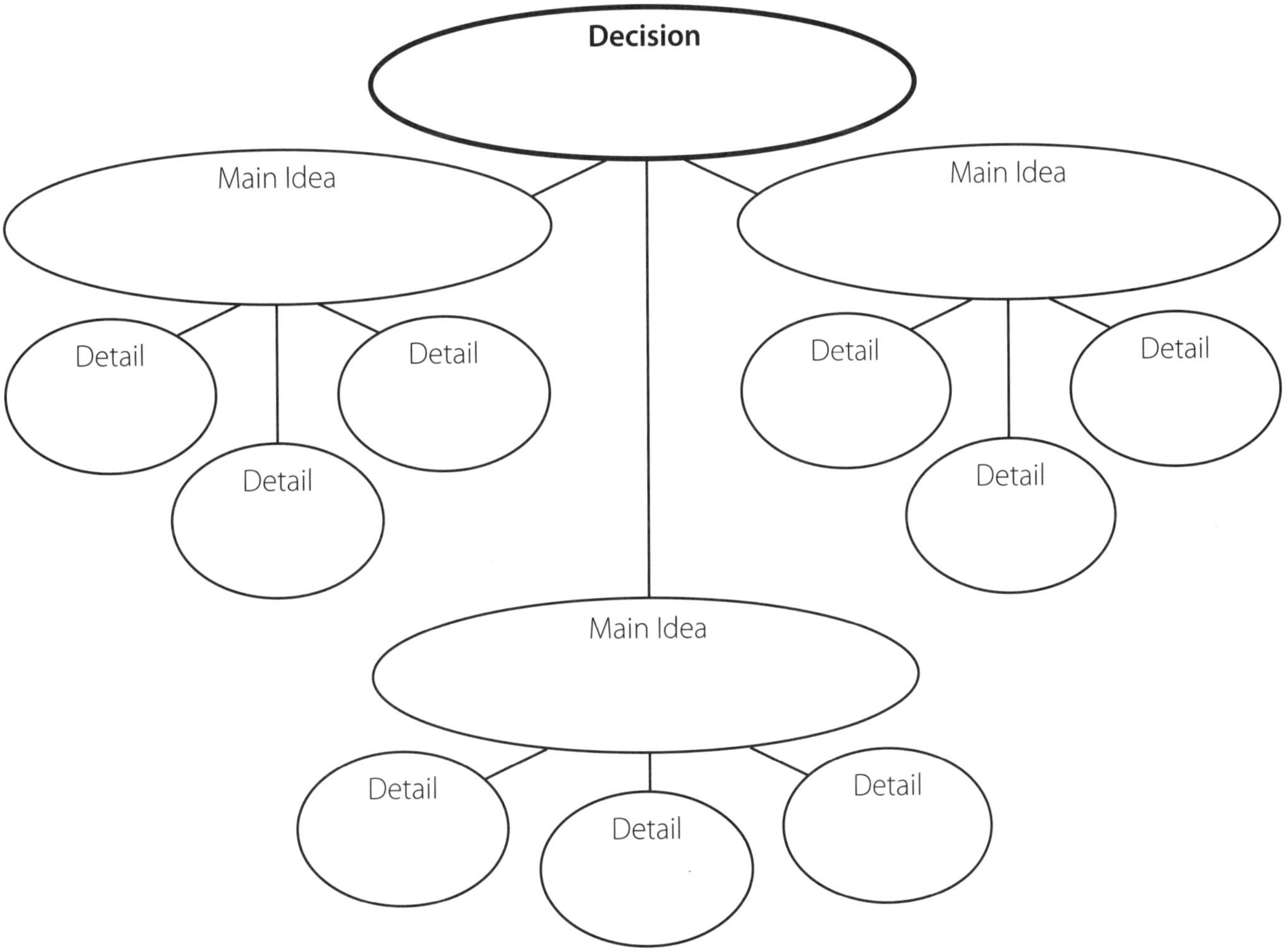

Write

On a separate piece of paper, write to your friend or mentor about the decision. Base the letter on your list of reasons for and against, and include information from the idea web you made.

Reread your letter. Then evaluate it against the rubric below. *In each row,* circle the statement that best describes your letter.

Feature	Well Done!	OK	Needs Work
Structure	Every main idea has its own paragraph and topic sentence.	Some paragraphs contain more than one main idea.	No clear main ideas in paragraphs.
Content	Letter presents specific details and clear reasons for and against the decision.	Reasons for and against the decision are presented, but not clearly. Some details.	Few details. Hard to follow the reasons for and against the decision.
Organization	Ideas are in logical, convincing order. Ideas flow smoothly from one to the next. Writer uses transition words well.	Idea sequence is a little confusing. Parts of the letter flow well, but other parts are jerky. Writer could make better use of transition words.	Ideas in no particular order. Ideas do not flow. Writer does not use transition words.

Did you circle statements under *OK* and *Needs Work?* Look under *Well Done!* in the same row to see how to improve your writing.

Revise

Extend your letter by answering the five W questions. Work with a writing partner.

1. Read your letter aloud to the partner.
2. Ask your partner to think like a newspaper writer, and ask several five W questions about your letter. What details have been left out? What else might a reader want to know? Write the questions below.

   Wh ____?

   Wh ____?

   Wh ____?

   Wh ____?

   Wh ____?

   H ____?

3. Choose one or two of the questions that interest you the most. Write notes about your answers. Where in your letter will you put this new information?

   ____

   ____

   ____

4. Revise your letter to include the additional details and any changes that you made after working with the rubric.

5. Work with a writing partner to evaluate your letter against this rubric. Decide together which statement *in each row* best describes your letter. Circle the statements.

Feature	Well Done!	OK	Needs Work
Audience	Audience is clear. Level of formality is right for the audience.	Audience is somewhat clear, but not always consistent.	Not clear that the writer has a specific audience in mind.
Structure	Every main idea has its own paragraph and topic sentence.	Some paragraphs contain more than one main idea.	No clear main ideas in paragraphs.
Content	Letter presents specific details and clear reasons for and against the decision.	Reasons for and against the decision are presented, but not clearly. Some details.	Few details. Hard to follow the reasons for and against the decision.
Organization	Ideas are in logical, convincing order. Ideas flow smoothly from one to the next. Writer uses transition words well.	Idea sequence is a little confusing. Parts of the letter flow well, but other parts are jerky. Writer could make better use of transition words.	Ideas in no particular order. Ideas do not flow. Writer does not use transition words.
Revision	New information fits well into the narrative flow.	New ideas have been added, but they aren't combined well with the earlier draft.	Very little change from original draft.

6. Did you circle statements under *OK* and *Needs Work?* Look under *Well Done!* in the same row to see how to improve your writing.

7. With your partner, review the Editing Checklist on page 93. Edit your letter, as needed. Check especially for the following:

    - agreement between subjects and verbs (Singular subject gets a singular verb; plural subject gets a plural verb.)
    - consistent verb tenses (present, past, future)
    - pronouns that clearly refer to someone or something

Produce and Present

Prepare a final version of your letter for your portfolio.

CHAPTER

7

Find the Support You Need

Writing Skill:
Adding Sensory Details

How many people start GED studies but get discouraged and quit? "I tried, but I couldn't do it," they say.

This could easily have happened to Wennik Watson, an Onondaga Native American. She had given up before. She studied with an Even Start tutor but didn't manage to stick with it.

Then, she re-enrolled. She still wanted to complete her GED. The problem? The writing test. She'd taken it twice but hadn't passed it.

This third time, Wennik graduated. Why? This time, Wennik found the right support.

Everyone needs support at one time or another. Finding it can make the difference between success and failure.

This is Wennik's story.

"I Wouldn't Have Finished Without Them."

Wennik's hands **trembled** as she opened the GED Testing Service letter. Had she passed the writing test she'd taken for the second time?

Not Pass. Wennik read the words, let out a long sigh, and closed her eyes. She wasn't sure if she was more disappointed for herself or for the teacher, friends, and family who had been helping her. But she was not going to let them down.

She called her teacher, Pattie. "I'm disappointed, but I'm not done," she said firmly. Wennik doubled her homework time. She took her writing assignments to work, where her co-workers could help her. Although not an **eager** reader, she read a book on writing. She met more often with Pattie. **Repeatedly,** they reviewed grammar and punctuation. Wennik wrote essay after essay.

Learning had always been a problem for Wennik. Her single mom had worked several jobs to support the family, so Wennik learned no preschool skills at home. In school, her skills were so low she felt **embarrassed.** Learning Support classes helped, but she still hated school. Wennik skipped classes, got in lots of trouble, ended up in a detention center, and then went to a foster home. Also, she was **diagnosed** as being seriously depressed.

At the age of 16, Wennik quit school to have a baby. She got a job working with **Alzheimer's** patients and found that she liked helping people. But with low skills, she had trouble completing patients' charts. She also needed a diploma to advance in her work.

Then, Wennik discovered the Even Start Family Literacy program. Her first teacher was helpful, but the bond between them wasn't strong enough to keep Wennik in the program. After a move to another town, she tried again. This time, she met Pattie. Pattie was so cheerful and encouraging that their study sessions became enjoyable and **productive.** In little more than two years with Pattie, Wennik's language score rose from the third-grade level to GED level. She passed her writing test on the third try!

Now, education is a priority in Wennik's home. Her children do well in school, and Wennik is on the School Improvement Team at their school.

Without Pattie's motivation and the strong support of others, Wennik says that these wonderful changes in her life would not have occurred.

Vocabulary

trembled – shook

eager – enthusiastic; impatient to do

repeatedly – over and over

embarrassed – uncomfortable or ashamed

diagnosed – recognized as having a disease or condition

Alzheimer's – degenerative disease of the central nervous system

productive – giving good results

Vocabulary Exercises

Read the two sentences aloud. Circle the one that makes more sense.

1.	He **embarrassed** the kitchen.	or	He was **productive** on that job.
2.	Her legs **diagnosed** on the diving board.	or	Her legs **trembled** on the diving board.
3.	She was an **eager** student.	or	She was a **repeatedly** student.
4.	Elisa's father has **Alzheimer's.**	or	Her husband has **eager.**
5.	The doctor **trembled** Elisa's father.	or	The doctor **diagnosed** the problem.
6	Angelo was late **repeatedly.**	or	Angelo got **Alzheimer's** lost.
7.	I was **embarrassed** by his language.	or	I was **productive** by his language.

Write the vocabulary word that best fits each sentence. Then read the sentences aloud.

8. What happened when Yan went to the doctor?

   He was ______________________ with the chicken pox.

9. What happened to the building during the earthquake?

   The building ______________________ and some windows broke.

10. Was Paul excited about his new car?

    He sure was! He was one very ______________________ driver!

11. Did the new father visit his baby often?

    Oh yes, he visited his wife and baby ______________________.

12. How did Katya feel after her presentation?

    She felt ______________________ about her mistake.

13. What is Dr. Han's research area?

    He studies elderly ______________________ patients and is working to find a cure.

14. What kind of a week did Fran have?

    She had a very ______________________ week.

React to the Story

Write about the story. For five minutes, write whatever comes to mind. Don't worry about details. Just write.

Writing Skill: Adding Sensory Details

Make your writing come alive by including sensory details—details related to the senses of hearing, smell, sight, touch, and taste. Here's an example. Which of the following passages makes you really feel the writer's fear?

> "The big dog growled and started chasing me. I ran as fast as I could."

> "The big dog showed his yellow fangs, snarled deep in his chest, and raced towards me. As I fled, I heard his snapping jaws and pounding feet behind me, gaining every second."

Write at least four words from the second passage that tell what the writer heard or saw:

Use details like these to engage your reader's senses.

Stories are usually told in time order. What happened first? What happened second? Then what happened? A story time line like the diagram below can help you organize what you want to say in a story.

Three pigs build houses.	▶	Wolf destroys straw house.	▶	Wolf destroys wooden house.	▶	Wolf can't destroy brick house.	▶	Pigs live happily in brick house.

Get Ready to Write

Assignment

Tell an exciting story to a child or a friend.

Think of a time when you felt great emotion. Perhaps you were extremely happy or terrified or shocked, etc. You are going to tell a story about why you felt that way. You'll tell, or **narrate,** the story to a child or a friend.

1. Brainstorm possible stories. Then select the best one to tell a child or your friend.

2. Think about specific events in the story. What happened first? Second? Third? Put the main events into a story time line in the boxes below. If you need more boxes, use another piece of paper.

1.	2.	3.	4.	5.

3. Search your memory for details of what you saw, heard, smelled, tasted, or touched in each part of the story. Make notes about those details.

Sights	Sounds	Smells	Tastes	Textures

4. Number the sensory details to show where they fit in the story. Use the numbers of the boxes in the story time line.

5. Think about how you can move from one part of the story to the next. You will need to use transition words to lead readers through the events smoothly. Transition words that show time order include these:

first	during	when
next	before	as soon as
then	soon	meanwhile
later	until	

6. You will need several paragraphs to tell your story. Remember to write each paragraph around one main event or point and to start a new paragraph when you change to a new point or event.

Write

1. Write your story on another piece of paper.

2. Review your first draft, using the rubric below. *In each row,* circle the statement that best fits your story.

Feature	Well Done!	OK	Needs Work
Audience	Story is written to appeal to its audience.	Not clear for which audience the story is written.	Story is inappropriate for its audience.
Structure	Well-structured story with a clear beginning, middle, and ending.	Opening does not grab reader's attention. Ending feels incomplete.	Events have no clear beginning or ending.
Content	Story is full of specific sensory details that bring the experience to life.	The writer includes many details, but they don't convey the emotional content.	The story has few details; those it does have do not engage the reader.
Organization	Story moves smoothly from an interesting beginning to an engaging middle to a satisfying end.	Sometimes hard to follow time sequence.	Story does not flow. Time sequence seems to jump around.
Word Choice	The story uses specific nouns and verbs, and colorful adjectives.	The story uses common, general, and less interesting words.	Vague, overused words make the story seem boring.

3. Did you circle statements under *OK* and *Needs Work?* Look under *Well Done!* in the same row to see how to improve your writing.

Revise

1. Tell your story to a writing partner. Ask your partner whether he or she understood the sequence of events. Do you need to reorder any parts of your story? If so, make notes on the first draft.

2. Talk with your partner about the sensory details that you have included. Can you think of any words that would describe them in a stronger way? Make notes about wording that would improve your story.

3. Use one of the questioning techniques (page 32 or page 34) to identify details that would make the story better. On your first draft, make notes about details you want to add.

4. Write a final draft of your story. Make sure it flows smoothly in time order and brings the experience to life with sensory details.

5. Work with a writing partner to evaluate your story against this rubric. Decide together which statement *in each row* best describes your story. Circle the statements.

Feature	Well Done!	OK	Needs Work
Audience	Story is written to appeal to its audience.	Not clear for which audience the story is written.	Story is inappropriate for its audience.
Structure	Well structured story with a clear beginning, middle, and ending.	Opening does not grab reader's attention. Ending feels incomplete.	Events have no clear beginning or ending.
Content	Story is full of specific sensory details that bring the experience to life.	The writer includes many details, but they don't convey the emotional content.	The story has few details; those it does have do not engage the reader.
Organization	Story moves smoothly from an interesting beginning to an engaging middle to a satisfying end.	Sometimes hard to follow time sequence.	Story does not flow. Time sequence seems to jump around.
Word Choice	The story uses specific nouns and verbs and colorful adjectives.	The story uses common, general, and less interesting words.	Vague, overused words make the story seem boring.
Revision	New information improves the story and is smoothly combined with original draft.	New information not combined well with the story.	Very little change in revised story. Changes stand out.

Discuss with your writing partner what you could do to improve your rating.

With your writing partner, check your revised story against the Editing Checklist on page 93. Make necessary edits to the story.

Produce and Present

Prepare a final copy of the story for your portfolio.

Stories are fun to share. Try one or more of these ideas:

- Illustrate your story and give it to a child or a friend.
- Put your illustrated story on a poster and display it.
- Create a class book of stories. Give copies to class members.
- Have a class storytelling session. Invite families and friends.

CHAPTER

8

Keep a Positive Outlook

Writing Skill:
Summarizing

Daniel Juárez thought he had good reasons for not completing his high-school education. But when events forced him to return to school, Daniel realized his reasons had really just been excuses.

Once he returned to the classroom, Daniel learned a lot more than English and math. He learned that if he was willing to work hard, he could make his dream come true. He learned that he was not very likely to get what he wanted in life by thinking, *This is too hard. I just can't do it.*

Daniel's experiences with school changed his whole outlook on life. He now believes in himself. He knows that if he sets a goal, he can reach it. "Anything is possible," he says, "if you stay focused and don't give up. It won't be easy, but if you keep a positive outlook, you can make it happen. No one can do it for you. You must do it by yourself, for yourself."

This is Daniel's story.

"No Excuses!"

Daniel Juárez dropped out of his high school in Mexico to come to the United States. He often thought about completing his high-school education, but soon he was very busy with a full-time restaurant job and a young family. There just didn't seem to be time for school.

All that changed one night when he told his boys to do their homework. One asked, "Why do I need to go to school? You didn't finish."

Daniel was crushed. Was he a bad **influence** on his sons? That night, he tossed and turned in bed.

The next day, Daniel signed up for evening classes, which he attended every night for months. He was tired both working and going to school, but he wanted to succeed for his sons. Over time, Daniel's English improved **enormously,** and he earned his GED!

When Daniel stopped to thank his teacher, Laurie, for her help, she said, "You can't stop now. You have too much **potential!**"

College had never crossed his mind. He was ready for a break from his **hectic** schedule. "I don't have the money," he told Laurie. "And I'd never be home at night with my family." But Laurie knew Daniel had always wanted to be a chef. She convinced him to tour a nearby culinary arts program at a community college.

Daniel visited the college and completed financial aid forms. A few weeks later, he was admitted to the program and received a grant that would pay for all of his expenses!

He was going to be a chef! Daniel felt **fortunate** that his excuses hadn't stood in his way. His family was thrilled for him and very proud of his accomplishment.

Attending college and working at the same time was **arduous.** Sometimes, he was so exhausted that tears would roll down his face as he drove from work to classes. But he wouldn't quit. *I can do this. I just have to keep telling myself that.*

Now, Daniel visits other classes to share his **positive** outlook and to give others hope. "If you want something, it's up to you to make it happen. No excuses!"

Vocabulary

influence – a person that has an effect on another person

enormously – in a big way

potential – ability not yet used

hectic – very busy

fortunate – lucky

arduous – difficult; hard

positive – confident; optimistic; encouraging

Vocabulary Exercises

Circle the correct word.

1. If you haven't had a chance to sit down all day, is your schedule **hectic** or **potential?**
2. Does Daniel find his working/studying life **arduous** or **influence?**
3. Is Daniel's attitude in life **arduous** or **positive?**
4. Will Daniel's job opportunities grow **hectic** or **enormously?**
5. Would you say Daniel has **potential** in his field or **fortunate** in his field?
6. Did Daniel feel **fortunate** or **enormously** when he began chef's training?
7. Does Daniel want to be an **influence** on others, or does he want to be a **positive** on them?

To answer each question, write a full sentence using an appropriate vocabulary word.
Then read the sentences aloud.

8. How would you describe your busy schedule? ______________________________

   ____

9. What is it like to work and go to school at the same time? ______________________________

   ____

10. How would you describe your attitude? ______________________________

    ____

11. Have your reading skills improved a great deal? ______________________________

    ____

12. Would you be able to do well in a culinary arts program? ______________________________

    ____

13. When do you feel lucky? ______________________________

    ____

14. In what way would you like to affect how someone thinks? ______________________________

    ____

React to the Story

Write about the story. For five minutes, write whatever comes to mind. Don't worry about details. Just write.

Writing Skill: Summarizing

So far, the chapters in this book have encouraged you to increase the amount of information in your writing: Add details! Explain more fully!

However, this chapter will require you to write less, to **summarize** a story. A good summary includes the main points in each section of the original work. It combines these ideas in a way that makes sense but that is much shorter than the original.

Here is an example. First, reread Richard's story on page 14. Now, read this summary of his story. Does it cover all the most important ideas?

> As a child, Richard hated school. He dropped out before he graduated from high school. Although he found a good job, he had many problems, including trouble with alcohol and drugs.
>
> Richard went into a treatment program and realized that he wanted to read and write better. So he entered a literacy program, where his learning difficulty was diagnosed. Knowing what the problem was, he was able to figure out learning methods that worked for him.
>
> With encouragement from his teacher, Richard overcame his fear of school and went to college. It was hard, but, in time, he graduated. Today, he teaches and counsels people with learning disabilities.

Get Ready to Write

Assignment

Summarize Daniel's story, as if you were going to include a short article about him in a newsletter.

Write three short paragraphs—first a beginning, then the middle, and finally a conclusion. Each paragraph should have three or fewer sentences.

1. Identify no more than ten of the most important ideas from Daniel's story. An idea may be stated in one sentence, or it may be expressed in several sentences. Write your list of the most important ideas below, using your own words.

2. Compare your list with the lists of your group or writing partner. Be ready to explain why you chose the ideas on your list. Discuss the lists as a group. Agree on the most important ideas in the story. Write them below.

3. Put a 1 beside the ideas that you will include in your beginning paragraph. Put a 2 beside the ideas that you will put into the middle paragraph. Then put a 3 beside the ideas that belong in the last paragraph.

Write

1. Write your three-paragraph summary.

    - Use your own words. Don't copy sentences from the story.
    - Try to capture the overall meaning, not specific details.
    - Make sure the summary has a beginning, a middle, and an end.
    - Use transition words to make the summary flow smoothly.

2. Read your summary aloud to the group. Listen to the summaries that others wrote.

   - Which summary includes all the most important ideas in the smallest space?
   - Which summary sounds most natural? Why?

Revise

Decisions about what to include in a summary and what to omit from a summary can be difficult. The shorter the summary, the more difficult the decisions become.

1. Rewrite your **three-paragraph** summary into a **five-sentence summary.** The summary must still make sense, even though it will contain only some of the story's main ideas. Be sure each sentence is complete.

2. Evaluate each of your summaries against this rubric. *In each row,* circle the statement that best describes your work. Use different colors for the two summaries.

Feature	Well Done!	OK	Needs Work
Structure—Original Summary	Three paragraphs, each no more than three sentences long.	More paragraphs or more sentences than specified.	Writer does not follow assignment guidelines.
Structure—Revised Summary	One paragraph of five sentences.	More sentences than specified.	Writer does not follow assignment guidelines.
Content	Summary covers overall meaning of story.	Summary picks up good details, but overall meaning is not clear.	Summary is made up of unrelated details. Overall meaning is lost.
Organization	Summary flows smoothly from beginning to end.	Flow is interrupted. Events are strung together without transition words.	Summary does not flow. Hard to understand sequence.
Word Choice	Writer uses own words to condense the story without losing critical information.	Some important information is still in original author's words.	Critical information has been lost in the summary. Writer does not use own words.

Did you circle statements under *OK* and *Needs Work?* Look under *Well Done!* in the same row to see how to improve your writing.

3. As a group, review the original and revised summaries written by all class members.

 - Read the original summaries aloud. Which ones sound best? Look at those summaries carefully. How did the writers make them flow so well?
 - Look for the shortest summaries. Did they include all the important ideas? If so, how did the writers make them so short?
 - Look at the revised, five-sentence summaries. When a summary is this short, important details must be left out. Which ideas survived? Did everyone keep the same details?

Produce and Present

Make final copies of both summaries to put in your portfolio.

CHAPTER 9

The Power of Education

Writing Skill:
Sequencing

Ramona Linan and her 12 family members had always worked in the fields. Fieldwork wasn't a bad way to make a living, but Ramona wanted her daughters to have choices in life. How could she make that happen?

Things began to change when Ramona enrolled in an English class. This proved to be an exhausting undertaking, since she had to clean offices all night in order to attend classes during the day. And she was also a single mom caring for two little girls.

But Ramona was persistent. Not only did she improve her English, but she also earned her GED. However, she realized that she needed more education to get the kind of job that would earn a good living for her family. But college? Never had she even considered such a thing.

Ramona's desire for education would bring about miracles in her family's life, a perfect example of the power of education.

This is Ramona's story.

"My Children Will Have a Better Life!"

Putting her young daughter to bed one night, Ramona Linan was **dismayed** to hear, "Mama, cuando yo sea grande, yo quiero trabajar en el campo como tú y mi abuelita." (Mommy, when I am older, I want to work in the fields like you and my grandmother.) These words rang over and over in Ramona's mind.

Ramona wanted more **options** for her girls. The only way she knew to begin was to enroll in English classes.

Even though her husband, Jaime, disapproved, Ramona was determined to build a future for her girls. That winter, she started school. She loved her classes, but the fieldwork season soon approached. Her teacher, Cathy Jo, helped Ramona find a nighttime cleaning job so she could earn money and still keep her days free for classes. However, Ramona had separated from her husband. He had begun using drugs and was eventually jailed. This meant Ramona was now a single parent, working full-time and going to school. Life was exhausting.

Nevertheless, Ramona studied hard. Within a year, she passed the Spanish version of the GED test. However, she realized that she would need more education to get a job that would support her family.

Cathy Jo wanted Ramona to go on a tour of a nearby community college. Even thinking of college was scary for Ramona because she had completed only six years of formal schooling. But the tour turned out to be the doorway to a dream. How had she forgotten her childhood desire to become a nurse? Knowing that she would still have to work full-time, Ramona **estimated** that it would take ten years for her to become a registered nurse.

She enrolled in a "bridge class," which helped her make the **transition** to college. The counselors and teachers were encouraging. Ten years later, Ramona reached her goal! She graduated with a nursing degree and began to work in a **rehabilitation** center.

Was it worth it? Two miracles in her family life answer that question. First, her daughters are college bound, and one decided that she wanted to become a doctor! And second, Ramona and her husband got back together. He earned a college degree in sociology, and he now works with troubled youths. Ramona was thrilled to have been such an **inspiration** to her family!

Education can transform lives.

Vocabulary

dismayed – not sure how to deal with something; upset

options – choices

nevertheless – in spite of that

estimated – made a careful guess

transition – change; the passage from one stage to another

rehabilitation – restoring to good health

inspiration – courageous example or influence

Vocabulary Exercise

Write the vocabulary word that best fits each sentence. Then complete the open sentences. Read the sentences aloud.

1. It can be hard to make the ____________________ from high school to college.

   The city girl enjoyed making the ____________________ to country life.

   Transition means ____.

2. Accident victims often have to go to ____________________ centers for physical therapy.

   Ramona became a nurse in a ____________________ facility.

   Rehabilitation means ____.

3. Ramona's hard work was an ____________________ to her family.

   Mrs. Cena looked to her grandmother for ____________________.

   Inspiration means ____.

4. Ramona was always tired. ____________________, she studied hard.

   Touring the campus was scary for Ramona. ____________________, she did it.

   Nevertheless means ____.

5. An artist has more career ____________________ in a city than in a small town.

   Having a GED or high-school diploma will increase your job ____________________.

   Options are ____.

6. The driver ____________________ that the trip would take eight hours.

   The policeman ____________________ that the car skidded for about 100 feet.

   Estimated means ____.

7. The father was ____________________ at the sight of his daughter's messy room.

   I was ____________________ when I heard about the accident.

   Dismayed means ____.

React to the Story

Write about the story. For five minutes, write whatever comes to mind. Don't worry about details. Just write.

Writing Skill: Sequencing

When you write, your sentences are always in some order. But if you don't think about sequence, the order that you use may not make sense or may be less effective than it could be.

Sometimes you need to sequence carefully, to organize your sentences in the most effective order for a particular purpose. Here are a few of the many sequencing options. When might you use each one?

- time order (yesterday, today, tomorrow)
- order of importance (most to least important, least to most important)
- location order (on the left, in the middle, on the right)
- order of difficulty (easiest to hardest; hardest to easiest)
- order by category (group 1, group 2, etc.)
- order by cost (least to most expensive, most to least expensive)

Reread Ramona's story. What order is used in this story?

Get Ready to Write

Assignment

Sometimes, people can't attend formal classes. Create a flyer that reminds people of informal ways they can learn in their everyday lives.

Knowledge and education can be powerful pathways to a person's dreams. Even when people can't attend classes, there are still many ways for them to educate themselves.

1. With a writing partner or with the class as a whole, brainstorm a list of learning activities that do not involve formal classes.

2. From the list, choose at least six of your favorite ideas.

Write

Write two paragraphs about your list of ideas.

Revise

Create a flyer that might convince community members to use some of your suggestions.

1. Share the paragraphs you wrote with your partner or class.
2. With your partner or class, make a master list of ideas.
3. Where will you send your flyer? Choose a specific community audience.
4. On your own, select ideas from the master list that you will use in your flyer. Keep your community audience in mind as you choose. What would be most helpful to those readers?

   ______________________ ______________________

   ______________________ ______________________

   ______________________ ______________________

5. How will you sequence your ideas? Choose the method which will make your flyer the most persuasive to its readers. Here are some suggestions. You may think of others.

   - most important ideas first, then less important ones
   - easier strategies first, then harder ones
   - free activities first, then ones that cost money
   - activities in the home first, then activities outside the home
   - activities for parents, then activities for people without children
   - summer activities first, then ideas for winter or bad weather

   List your ideas, using the sequencing method you have chosen.

   1. ______________________ 4. ______________________

   2. ______________________ 5. ______________________

   3. ______________________ 6. ______________________

6. Write a title and a one- or two-sentence introduction for your flyer.

   ____

   ____

   ____

7. Write a one- or two-sentence conclusion for your flyer.

   ____

   ____

8. Write your flyer.

9. Reread your flyer. Then, evaluate it against this rubric. *In each row,* circle the statement that best describes your flyer.

Feature	Well Done!	OK	Needs Work
Audience	The flyer will be very useful to its specific audience.	Not clear which specific part of the community the flyer is meant to help.	Flyer doesn't seem to be designed for any particular audience.
Content	Interesting ideas that make sense for the audience.	Idea choice is OK, but could be a better fit for audience.	Ideas are not well matched to audience.
Organization	Idea sequence is effective and fits the specific audience.	Sequence of ideas is OK.	Ideas aren't in any particular order.
Mechanics	No errors in spelling, grammar, punctuation, or capitalization.	Few errors in spelling, grammar, punctuation, or capitalization.	Many errors in mechanics.

Did you circle statements under *OK* and *Needs Work?* Look under *Well Done!* in the same row to see how to improve your writing.

10. Pass around the flyers that members of the class have produced.

- Compare the ways in which flyers are organized. How many different sequencing methods were used? Ask writers why they chose their specific methods.
- Identify the parts of the flyers that are most effective. What makes those parts work so well?

Produce and Present

Make a final copy of your flyer to put in your portfolio.

Create a class flyer by combining the best ideas from all of the flyers.

- Choose the most effective sequencing method.
- Think about where to put each idea or group of ideas on the flyer page.
- Type the information, or have someone with excellent handwriting write it.
- Edit carefully for correct spelling and grammar.
- Then, make copies and distribute them in your community.

CHAPTER

10

Find Work You Love

Writing Skill:
Writing Essays

Tom Henneman was a drug and alcohol addict for most of his life. As he got older, he no longer cared whether he lived or died. Then the kind words of a stranger made him want to change. But would he be able to?

Many times during Tom's recovery, he felt like giving up. The effort to stay strong was harder than anything he'd ever done. What kept him going? There were two things. Tom had newfound religious faith. He also had a new goal, something he wanted more than anything else in his entire life.

He wanted to become a drug and alcohol counselor. If he shared the details of his troubled past with others, then perhaps they would make wiser choices than he had made. He couldn't wait to get to work.

This is Tom's story.

"It's the Only Way My Life Makes Sense."

"Come on, buddy, into the car," said the cop, as he pulled the drunk up off the alley pavement.

As they rode, the policeman said something to Tom that changed his life. "You seem like a nice guy. Do you suppose you need some help?"

Tom was tired of destroying his body. He was tired of having no permanent home. He'd been wandering since he'd left home at 16. The truth was that Tom no longer cared if he lived or died.

The next day, Tom entered a residential treatment facility. For one month, he went to meetings and **unburdened** his heart by writing in a journal. He wrote about growing up as one of 12 children. There had been a lot of drinking in his house. He also wrote of his embarrassment at not having a high-school diploma. His first step toward recovery would be to get that diploma. Then Tom had an **inspiration:** Perhaps he could become a drug and alcohol counselor. Helping others to avoid his mistakes would make his life make sense.

But first, he had to stay sober. Each clean day was a victory. His faith and his goal **propelled** him through those first long and hard months.

Tom enrolled in an adult education class. But on the night of the first class, he was almost too scared to go through the door. *I'll just make a fool of myself! I'm crazy to go back to the classroom!* But his dream—and his life—depended upon it.

Tom's fears soon eased. The teachers and students welcomed him. No one looked down on him for his past. Best of all, Tom found that he loved learning! In high school, his grades had been **mediocre.** Now, he worked hard and did well. Tom's progress made it easier to avoid drugs and drinking. Every day it became clearer that his goal was **attainable.**

Tom did become a drug and alcohol counselor! Many of the troubled teens with whom he now works are **sullen** or **defiant.** But some of them thank Tom after listening to his story. Tom knows that he has made them aware of the choices that they are making in their own lives.

Tom is living his dream. He says that without his faith and the goal of helping people, he would not have been able to make such progress in his life. By helping to save the lives of others, he has also saved his own.

Vocabulary

unburdened – freed from a heavy load

inspiration – brilliant, surprising idea

propelled – pushed forward as if driven

mediocre – not very good, but not terrible

attainable – possible to get or accomplish

sullen – showing anger by refusing to speak

defiant – angrily refusing to obey; ready to fight

Vocabulary Exercises

Write the vocabulary word that best fits each sentence. Then read the sentences aloud.

1. The teenager became silent and ______________________ when his mother wouldn't buy him the sneakers that he wanted.
2. The woman ______________________ her mind by talking to her sister.
3. Mia couldn't think of a solution, but then she had an ______________________.
4. Her Spanish was just ______________________, so she couldn't understand what he said.
5. His goal would be ______________________ only if he first passed his GED.
6. The ______________________ girl stomped out of the room and slammed the door.
7. The baby ______________________ himself across the room by rolling over and over.

Write the vocabulary word that makes sense in each sentence. Then read the sentences aloud.

8. An employee who does just enough to get by is considered a ______________________ worker.
   (defiant / mediocre)
9. I was ______________________ forward by the crowd that was trying to see the movie star.
   (propelled / unburdened)
10. When her parents said no to her request, she became ______________________.
    (sullen / mediocre)
11. Marta had a sudden ______________________. Now she knew what to do!
    (attainable / inspiration)
12. The ______________________ man yelled at the crowd and raised his fist.
    (defiant / sullen)
13. Tom ______________________ his mind by writing in his journal.
    (propelled / unburdened)
14. The counselor showed him that his goals were ______________________.
    (attainable / inspiration)

React to the Story

Write about the story. For five minutes, write whatever comes to mind. Don't worry about details. Just write.

____

____

____

____

____

____

____

____

____

____

Writing Skill: Writing Essays

Just as a good story has a beginning, a middle part, and an end, an essay needs an introduction, a body, and a conclusion.

The **introduction** tells the reader about your topic and may mention your main ideas. For example:

> Because I am a city girl, one of my favorite weekend activities is taking long walks in the country. It's a whole new world for me to explore. And being surrounded by the sights and sounds of nature, even for a short time, brings me a kind of peace I don't experience in the busy rush of city life.

Body paragraphs contain the essay's main ideas and the details that support them. The introduction above leads the reader to expect two body paragraphs. The first paragraph would explain the "new world" the author finds on her walks. The second paragraph would discuss the peaceful feeling that she gets when she is in the countryside. See pages 5–12 to review how body paragraphs should be constructed.

Instead of stopping suddenly at the end of the last body paragraph, an essay is brought to a close by a **conclusion.** The conclusion can be a summary of major points, or it can make a final statement that emphasizes the writer's viewpoint. For example:

> After a one- or two-hour country walk, I return to the city totally content. The exercise has revived me, and I'm excited about what I've seen in the natural world. My spirit is refreshed because the strange sights and sounds have pushed away my daily worries. For me, nature's paths bring peace.

Get Ready to Write

Assignment

In essay form, describe a favorite activity to an adviser or a mentor.

Tom was able to change his life because he found work that he really wanted to do. At first, Tom didn't have the skills and the training that he needed to do the job. But because his goal meant so much to him, he was able to stay focused and get the training and the skills that he lacked.

What kind of work would you like to do? Think of a moment when you've been so busy with an activity that time just flew by. When you looked at the clock, you thought, "Where did the time go?" Could you turn a favorite activity into satisfying work?

1. Make a list of activities that you really enjoy or are eager to try. If possible, discuss your list with classmates or friends. Do they help you think of more ideas?

____

____

____

____

2. Choose one activity from your list. Use the chart to list specific details that describe this activity and why it interests you.

Activity: ____

Who	What	Where	When	Why	How

3. Decide how to organize your thoughts for the essay. In the space below, make an idea map or group ideas by paragraph (list all the ideas for the first paragraph, then all the ideas for the second paragraph, etc.). Plan two to four body paragraphs. Don't worry about the introduction or conclusion at this time.

Write

1. Write two to four body paragraphs describing the activity to a mentor or an adviser.

Reread your body paragraphs. Then evaluate them against this rubric. *In each row,* circle the statement that best describes your paragraphs.

Feature	Well Done!	OK	Needs Work
Structure	Ideas organized into effective paragraphs. Each presents its main idea in a topic sentence.	Ideas are good, but not well organized. Each paragraph has one main idea; no topic sentences.	Ideas are poorly organized. No clear main ideas in paragraphs.
Content	Interesting and specific details support each main idea.	Paragraph details could be more specific and interesting.	Details often unrelated to main points.
Organization	Moves smoothly from paragraph to paragraph.	Some transitions are awkward.	Transitions between paragraphs are poor or missing.
Word Choice	Writer uses specific, interesting words appropriate for an adviser or a mentor.	Words are appropriate for the audience, but not very interesting.	Writer chooses obvious and overused words. Some words do not fit the audience.

What specific changes can you make to your paragraphs to improve your rating on the rubric?

Revise

1. Plan your introductory paragraph. How will you focus your reader's attention on the body paragraphs that you have written?

2. Plan your conclusion. How will you summarize your points and bring the essay to a satisfying stopping point?

3. On a separate piece of paper, revise your essay.

   - Include the introduction and the conclusion that you have planned. Make sure that the new parts fit smoothly into your essay.
   - Revise the body paragraphs as suggested by your rubric review.
   - Use the Editing Checklist on page 93 to help you make final edits.

4. Work with a writing partner to evaluate your essay against this rubric. Decide together which statement *in each row* best describes your essay. Circle the statements.

Feature	Well Done!	OK	Needs Work
Structure	Ideas organized into effective paragraphs. Each presents its main idea in a topic sentence.	Ideas are good, but not well organized. Each paragraph has one main idea; no topic sentences.	Ideas are poorly organized. No clear main ideas in paragraphs.
Content	Interesting and specific details support each main idea.	Paragraph details could be more specific and interesting.	Details often unrelated to main points.
Organization	Moves smoothly from paragraph to paragraph.	Some transitions are awkward.	Transitions between paragraphs are poor or missing.
Word Choice	Writer uses specific, interesting words appropriate for an adviser or a mentor.	Words are appropriate for the audience, but not very interesting.	Writer chooses obvious and overused words. Some words do not fit the audience.
Revision	Introduction and conclusion are effective and well integrated.	Introduction and conclusion are present but not well integrated.	No clear introduction or conclusion.
Mechanics	No errors in grammar and mechanics.	A few errors in grammar or mechanics.	Many errors in grammar or mechanics.

Discuss with your writing partner what you could do to improve your writing.

Produce and Present

Prepare a final version of your essay for your portfolio.

Consider showing your essay to your adviser or mentor. It might start a useful discussion about your future plans.

CHAPTER 11

The Good Life

Writing Skill:
Cohesive Writing

Bernardino Alvarez, one of ten children, had to leave school after the sixth grade to help support his family. He worked in the Mexican potato fields for ten years. Then, he became a carpenter's assistant. He grew skilled and joined with his brothers to begin a carpentry business. But in 1995, the Mexican economy collapsed. His business went under, and Bernardino was left with nothing except unpaid taxes. He saw no choice but to leave his family and try to find work in the United States.

Bernardino had been poor most of his life, but at least he had been at home with his loved ones. In Philadelphia, PA, he was not only penniless but also alone. The new language and customs were confusing. Bernardino was starving, jobless, and afraid of being arrested as an illegal immigrant. It was a terrifying time.

However, with much luck, the kindness of strangers, and hard work, Bernardino survived. After finally settling in, he was amazed at the many opportunities he found in his new country. Could he take advantage of them and build a good life for himself and his family? Or was that just a foolish dream?

This is Bernardino's story.

"Tomorrow Will Be Better for Me."

Toward the end of Bernardino's first day at his new job in his new country, he was so hungry that he was on the **verge** of passing out. **Desperately,** he made eating motions to his co-workers.

They rushed to a grocery store. The food that they bought for him to eat made him feel very sick, or perhaps he felt sick because of the worry, fear, and confusion. He was an **illegal** immigrant and spoke almost no English. Would he be put in jail? Could he survive with no money? Perhaps his plan was **unrealistic.** But he couldn't go back to Mexico. There was no way for him to earn a living for his family there.

He had to do this. *Tomorrow will be better for me,* he told himself.

Bernardino was back on the job the next morning, still sick, still fearful, and still overwhelmed by the new language and customs. That night, as he began to do every night, he told himself, *Tomorrow will be better for me.*

Eventually, tomorrow was better. His boss liked Bernardino's hard work and admired his **carpentry** skills. He could see that Bernardino was struggling to survive, so he began to help him. He gave Bernardino rides to work and lent him money. Over time, he helped Bernardino find an apartment, get his working papers, enroll in English classes, and get a computer.

Classes at La Comunidad Hispaña changed Bernardino's life. He began in the level-one English class. Over the next five years, he progressed through all six levels. He went to work from 7:00 a.m. to 5:00 p.m., and then, without fail, attended classes every evening. With his teachers' encouragement, he earned his GED and studied computers. "I worked with all my power," says Bernardino. "It was exhausting, but I had to."

Now, life is good. Bernardino owns a successful **carpentry** business. He has brought his family members to join him in the United States. He enjoys **designing** houses and dreams of being an **architect.**

"I am happy now," Bernardino says. "Life is easier, and I am excited about the future."

Vocabulary

verge – edge

desperately – with great need and anxiety

illegal – against the law

unrealistic – unworkable; unlikely; not realistic

carpentry – related to building and repairing houses and other wooden things

designing – drawing plans for the form or structure of something

architect – a professional designer of buildings

Vocabulary Exercise

Write the vocabulary word that best fits each sentence. Then complete the open sentences. Read the sentences aloud.

1. Bernardino developed a successful ____________________ business.

   He learned his ____________________ skills while he was still in Mexico.

   Carpentry skills involve ____.

2. Is it legal or ____________________ in this state to turn right on a red light?

   Parking by a fire hydrant is ____________________.

   It is illegal to ____.

3. Joe won an award for ____________________ the best kitchen.

   Darlene's favorite activity is ____________________ fancy dresses.

   I like designing ____.

4. ____________________, the man dialed 911.

   Kueth has just arrived in the United States. He ____________________ needs a place to live.

   I desperately wanted ____.

5. The river was on the ____________________ of overflowing.

   His business is on the ____________________ of bankruptcy.

   I was on the verge of ____.

6. A famous ____________________ is designing the new courthouse.

   We met with the builder and the ____________________ yesterday.

   An architect designed ____.

7. Is it ____________________ to think that the world could support billions more people?

   Some politicians try to get votes by making ____________________ promises.

   It is unrealistic to ____.

React to the Story

Write about the story. For five minutes, write whatever comes to mind. Don't worry about details. Just write.

Writing Skill: Cohesive Writing

As you begin to write longer pieces and essays, make sure that your writing flows into one **cohesive** piece. In cohesive writing, the parts mesh smoothly and logically together, making it easy for a reader to follow your clearly stated ideas.

Reread Bernardino's story on page 86. With a writing partner, find the point at which the story moves from one section to another section. Where does it change from beginning to middle, and from middle to end? How do you know?

Write the first sentence of the story's middle.

Write the first sentence of the story's ending.

Write the transition words that begin each of the last two sections.

Using transition words well is the key to cohesive writing. They are the guideposts that lead the reader from idea to idea and from section to section.

Get Ready to Write

Assignment

Bernardino sees the United States as a land of opportunity. Do you agree with him? State your opinion in an essay. Give specific reasons to support your view.

1. First, think about the question. What are you being asked to do? This question specifically asks for **reasons** to support your **opinion.**
2. Discuss the question with a writing partner or group. Explain to each other why you think as you do.
3. Decide what opinion you will present. Write that opinion in the top box of the idea web below.
4. Why do you have this opinion? Write one reason for your opinion in each of the idea web's reason boxes. Choose convincing reasons to make the strongest argument you can.
5. Add any details and examples to the reason boxes.
6. How will you end the essay? Make notes in the conclusion box.

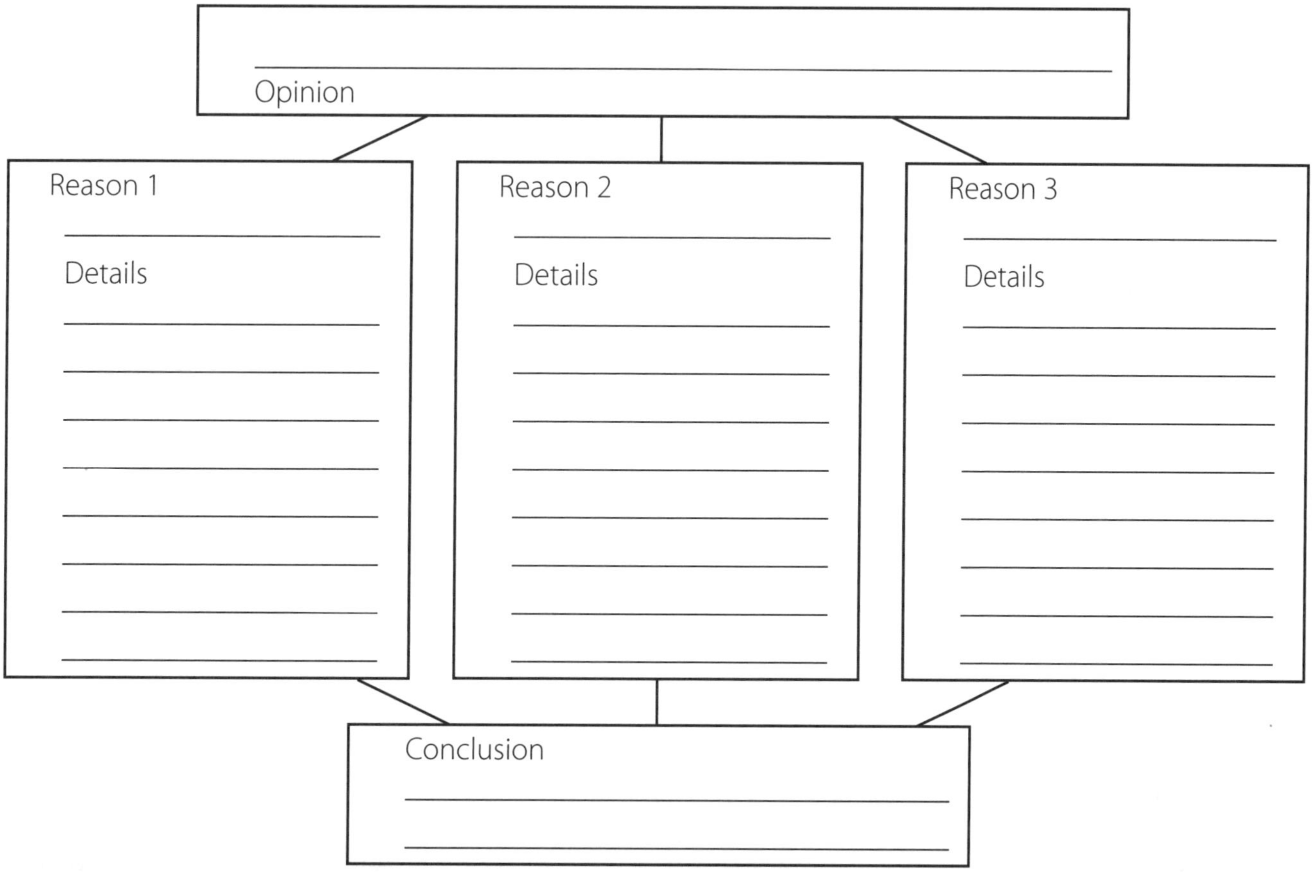

Write

Draft your essay on a separate piece of paper. Follow your idea web. Include an introduction, body paragraphs, and a conclusion.

Revise

1. Review what you have written.

   Keep your reader in mind. Will that person be able to follow your reasoning easily? If not, try to understand why.

   Reread your essay. Then evaluate it against this rubric. *In each row,* circle the statement that best describes your essay.

Feature	Well Done!	OK	Needs Work
Structure	Essay has an engaging introduction, several body paragraphs, and a strong conclusion. Every main idea has its own paragraph.	Introduction and conclusion are present, but not effective. Sometimes more than one main idea per paragraph.	No introduction or conclusion at all, just body paragraphs. No clear main ideas in paragraphs.
Organization	Ideas are in logical, convincing order. Essay flows smoothly from one idea to the next. Writer uses transition words well.	Idea sequence is a little confusing. Parts of the essay flow well, but other parts are jerky. Could use transition words better.	Ideas aren't in any particular order. Essay does not flow. Writer does not use transition words.
Content	Essay presents clear reasons for opinion supported by specific details. All details relate directly to reasons.	Reasons for opinion are presented, but not clearly. Details not specific.	Hard to follow the reasons for opinion. Details not related to main points.

   What specific changes can you make to your essay to improve your rating on the rubric?

2. Write a final version of your essay.

3. With a partner, edit your essay carefully. Use the Editing Checklist on page 93. Make changes on the essay itself.

4. This essay assignment is similar to the essay you will be asked to write if you take the GED Language Arts essay test. Try evaluating your essay against the GED Essay Scoring Rubric on page 94.

   - First, with the class or a partner, read through the GED Essay Scoring Rubric. How is it similar to the rubrics you have been using? How is it different?
   - Work with a partner. Review both of your essays against this rubric. *In each row,* decide together which statement best describes each of your essays. Circle it.
   - Although you may find it helpful to use the GED Essay Scoring Rubric in this way, people who score GED essay tests use the guide differently. They look at whole essays, not essay parts. Every essay is given just one score between 1 and 4 for the test. A 2 or higher is a passing score. With your partner, decide where on the GED scale your essays fall.

Produce and Present

Put a final copy of your essay into your portfolio.

With your class, discuss whether the United States is a land of opportunity. Tell the class why you hold your opinion. Give the reasons that you included in your essay. Listen to the opinions of others.

Consider gathering essays into a class booklet or a bulletin board display.

Last Word

Review the portfolio that you have created as you worked through this book. Notice your progress! You have been using the best method for learning to write well—writing, thinking about your writing, revising it, and then writing some more. Write! Revise! Succeed! May your writing skills help you to fulfill your dreams.

Editing Checklist

Mechanics

_____ I capitalized the first word in every sentence.

_____ I capitalized all proper nouns.

_____ Each sentence I wrote ends with a period, a question mark, or an exclamation point.

_____ I used punctuation correctly (commas, apostrophes, quotes, etc.).

_____ I spelled all words correctly. (Check carefully for commonly confused words like *they're, their, there; your, you're; its, it's*; etc.)

_____ I indented the beginning of each new paragraph.

Grammar

_____ Each of my sentences is a complete thought with a subject and a verb. There are no sentence fragments in my work.

_____ There are no run-on sentences that are incorrectly joined by commas.

_____ Subjects and verbs agree in number (singular subject, singular verb; plural subject, plural verb).

_____ When I use pronouns, they clearly refer to someone or something.

_____ I use verb tenses consistently unless a change is required (past, present, future).

Style

_____ I varied the lengths of sentences I wrote. Some are long, some are short, and some are medium in length.

_____ I chose clear, interesting, colorful, precise words and made sure that they were appropriate for my audience. I avoided vague, overused words and clichés.

_____ I cut out any unnecessary words. Nothing is more complicated than it needs to be.

GED Essay Scoring Rubric

	1	2	3	4
	Inadequate	**Marginal**	**Adequate**	**Effective**
	Reader has difficulty identifying or following the writer's ideas.	Reader occasionally has difficulty understanding or following the writer's ideas.	Reader understands the writer's ideas.	Reader understands and easily follows the writer's expression of ideas.
Response to the Prompt	Attempts to address prompt but with little or no success in establishing a focus.	Addresses the prompt, though the focus may shift.	Uses the writing prompt to establish a main idea.	Presents a clearly focused main idea that addresses the prompt.
Organization	Fails to organize ideas.	Shows some evidence of an organizational plan.	Uses an identifiable organizational plan.	Establishes a clear and logical organization.
Development and Details	Demonstrates little or no development; usually lacks the details or examples, or presents irrelevant information.	Has some development but lacks specific details; may be limited to a listing, repetitions or generalizations.	Has focused but occasionally uneven development; incorporates some specific detail.	Achieves coherent development with specific and relevant details and examples.
Conventions of Edited American English	Exhibits minimal or no control of sentence structure and the conventions of EAE.	Demonstrates inconsistent control of sentence structure and the conventions of EAE.	Generally controls sentence structure and the conventions of EAE.	Consistently controls sentence structure and the conventions of EAE.
Word Choice	Exhibits weak and/or inappropriate words.	Exhibits a narrow range of word choice, often including inappropriate selections.	Exhibits appropriate word choice.	Exhibits varied and precise word choice.

GED Testing Service. Reprinted with permission.

Glossary

accounting – keeping track of business finances
administrator – person in charge
Alzheimer's – degenerative disease of the central nervous system
analogies – test questions that compare relationships among words
anguished – filled with pain
architect – a professional designer of buildings
arduous – difficult; hard
asset – something positive that has value
attainable – possible to get or accomplish
blue-collar – describes work, often manual, that requires work clothes
browsed – skimmed; looked over casually
capable – able to do things well
carpentry – related to building and repairing houses and other wooden things
certified – officially approved
clientele – all of a business's customers together
conquer – overcome
credibility – believability; acceptance as being honest or true
culinary – related to cooking
debtor – a person who borrows money and must pay it back
defiant – angrily refusing to obey; ready to fight
designing – drawing plans for the form or structure of something
desperately – with great need and anxiety
diagnosed – recognized as having a disease or condition
discouraging – confidence reducing; depressing
dismayed – not sure how to deal with something; upset
downsized – cut to save the employer money
eager – enthusiastic; impatient to do
embarrassed – uncomfortable or ashamed
encouragement – support
enormously – in a big way
erupted – burst out
estimated – made a careful guess
exhausting – very tiring
facility – a building with a special purpose
fortunate – lucky
hectic – very busy
humiliate – shame or embarrass
illegal – against the law
immediately – right away; without delay
incident – brief, unplanned event
influence – a person that has an effect on another person
inspiration – brilliant, surprising idea
inspiration – courageous example or influence
investment – money or time spent in hope that it may pay off in the future
invisible – unable to be seen
liability – disadvantage or barrier
mediocre – not very good, but not terrible
mentor – teach; coach; advise; guide
milestone – important step toward a goal
mortgage – loan against property
nevertheless – in spite of that
nontraditional – not customary
notorious – famous for negative reasons
options – choices
overwhelmed – helpless; defeated
phobia – crippling fear
positive – confident; optimistic; encouraging
potential – ability not yet used
poverty – the state of being poor
precious – of great value
priority – something of great importance
procrastinate – keep putting off; delay
productive – giving good results
propelled – pushed forward as if driven
recipient – a person who gets something
recommended – suggested
rehabilitation – restoring to good health
repeatedly – over and over
residential – where people live
siblings – brothers and sisters
sullen – showing anger by refusing to speak
transformed – changed
transition – change; the passage from one stage to another
trembled – shook
unburdened – freed from a heavy load
unrealistic – unworkable; unlikely; not realistic
verge – edge
winced – made a brief movement in pain

Students and the Programs They Attended

Viridiana Ramos
Montebello Adult School
Montebello, CA

Richard Evans
Tom Green County Adult Literacy Council
San Angelo, TX

Jason Donaldson
Kennedy-King Community College Adult Education Program
Chicago, IL

Cynthia Brooks
GECAC and Stairways CareerLink GED
Erie, PA

LaDonna Taltoan
Lancaster Lebanon Intermediate Unit #13 Family Literacy Program
East Petersburg, PA

Arlene Cianelli
No program – self-study

Wennik Watson
Onondaga Cortland Madison BOCES GRASP Program
Liverpool, NY

Daniel Juárez
Hamilton – Fulton – Montgomery BOCES
Amsterdam, NY

Ramona Linan
Watsonville/Aptos Adult School
Watsonville, CA

Tom Henneman
Lassen Adult School
Susanville, CA

Bernardino Alvarez
La Comunidad Hispaña
Kennett Square, PA